SCOTT JOPLIN

BOOKS BY JAMES HASKINS

Biographies

RESISTANCE: Profiles in Nonviolence
REVOLUTIONARIES: Agents of Change
PROFILES IN BLACK POWER
A PIECE OF THE POWER: Four Black Mayors
FROM LEW ALCINDOR TO KAREEM ABDUL JABBAR
PINCKNEY BENTON STEWART PINCHBACK
RALPH BUNCHE: A Most Reluctant Hero
ADAM CLAYTON POWELL: Portrait of a Marching Black
BABE RUTH AND HANK AARON: The Home Run Kings
FIGHTING SHIRLEY CHISHOLM
DR. J.: A Biography of Julius Erving
THE STORY OF STEVIE WONDER
PELE
ALWAYS MOVIN' ON: The Life of Langston Hughes
THE LIFE AND DEATH OF MARTIN LUTHER KING, JR.
BARBARA JORDAN: Speaking Out

General Books

DIARY OF A HARLEM SCHOOLTEACHER
BLACK MANIFESTO FOR EDUCATION (Editor)
THE PSYCHOLOGY OF BLACK LANGUAGE, With Hugh F. Butts, M.D.
JOKES FROM BLACK FOLKS
WITCHCRAFT, MYSTICISM and MAGIC IN THE BLACK WORLD
STREET GANGS: Yesterday and Today
SNOW SCULPTURE AND ICE CARVING
A NEW KIND OF JOY: The Story of The Special Olympics
THE COTTON CLUB
THE GREAT AMERICAN CRAZIES, With Kathleen Benson and Ellen Inkelis

Juvenile Books

THE WAR AND THE PROTEST: Vietnam
RELIGIONS
THE CONSUMER MOVEMENT
THE PICTURE LIFE OF MALCOLM X
THE CREOLES OF COLOR OF NEW ORLEANS
YOUR RIGHTS: Past and Present
THE LONG STRUGGLE: The Story of American Labor

SCOTT JOPLIN

James Haskins
with Kathleen Benson

Doubleday & Company, Inc., Garden City, New York
1978

ISBN: 0-385-11155-x
Library of Congress Catalog Card Number 76–50768

CONTENTS

ACKNOWLEDGMENTS

This project has taken a period of years and has involved a number of people. I am extremely grateful to all of them, and I apologize to any person or institution that I have inadvertently failed to mention.

First, it is important to acknowledge those who have already published works or written original material on Scott Joplin: Vera Brodsky Lawrence, editor of *The Collected Works of Scott Joplin,* put me in touch with Dr. Addison Walker Reed, who did his unpublished doctoral thesis on Joplin; British author Peter Gammond published a book on Joplin that contains interesting insights into his music; and of course I am grateful to Rudi Blesh and Harriet Janis, whose *They All Played Ragtime* was the seminal work on ragtime and the life of Scott Joplin. Blesh and Janis were able to interview people who are now deceased, as were Ann Vanderlee, now deceased, and John Vanderlee of Fort Worth, Texas; their records are invaluable.

Acknowledgments

People in Texas and Arkansas were very helpful to me in establishing the facts and bases for speculation on Scott Joplin's early life. Jerry Atkins, Texarkana businessman and a prime force behind the move by the Texarkana Historical Society and Museum to establish its Scott Joplin collection and memorials, has been with me from the beginning, taking time to provide whatever material to which he had access and offering extremely helpful suggestions. Mrs. Arthur Jennings, chairman, Bowie County Historical Commission, provided a considerable amount of information on the Moores, Rochelle, Hooks and other families which helped to undergird my speculations on Jiles Joplin's early life in Texas. Her research and writings on the early days of Texarkana were also valuable. I am grateful as well to Fred Joplin and George Mosley, who remember Scott Joplin in Texarkana and who took the time to share their recollections. George Beasley and Burl Mitchell provided helpful information, as did Scott Joplin's niece, Mattie Harris; and Charles Steger of Longview, Texas, made the important discovery while searching through old census records of the presence of the Joplin family in Cass County, Texas, in 1870, when Scott was just two years old. I was helped immeasurably with my research in Texas by Dick J. Reavis, now of Austin; without him I could not have gathered nearly as much information as I did, and I am deeply grateful to him.

In researching Scott Joplin in Missouri, I was helped by Jan Goldberg, formerly of St. Louis, and by ragtime authority Trebor Jay Tichenor. Ms. Kathleen S. Schoene, librarian, and Miss Elizabeth Tindall, reference librarian, of the Missouri Historical Society and Mrs. Bonnie Ryck and her predecessor, Mrs. Debbie Miller, of the State Historical Society of Missouri, provided information in the form of old newspaper clippings and St. Louis City Directory entries, as did the staff of the Sedalia Public Library; county clerks' and vital records offices in a variety of Missouri counties searched vainly for various birth, death, and marriage records.

Lynn Bynum of Louisville, Kentucky, conducted an extensive search for records on Florence Givins Joplin and her family; Susan Baran made a similarly ambitious search of census records at the Schomburg Center for Research in Black Culture in Manhattan; also assisted in picture research. J. M. Stifle spent hours at the Lincoln Center branch of the New York Public Library; and Mr. Richard Jackson, curator of the American Music Collection at Lincoln Center, made efforts to establish a factual basis for the legend that Scott Joplin once visited Europe. In Nashville, Tennessee, Frank Benson and Jewel Moore gathered information from Fisk University's Samuel Brunson Campbell Papers. In New York City, members of the staff of the Museum of the City of New York provided old city directories and real estate records. Mary Ellen Arrington typed the manuscript drafts and provided helpful editorial comments.

All across the country, jazz buffs and Joplinophiles have been searching for information on Scott Joplin and readily sharing their discoveries with others in such publications as the *Rag Times*. I am indebted to all of them and hope that my work will provide continued impetus to their search.

I also wish to express my appreciation to the following individuals and institutions: Mr. James D. Walker of the National Archives, the Library of Congress, American Brands, Inc., the Department of State, New York City

Acknowledgments

Municipal Archives and Record Center, Ms. Margaret Scriven, librarian, Chicago Historical Society, the Texas General Land Office, the Texas State Library, the South Carolina Department of Archives and History, and the Missouri Pacific Railroad.

A special thank-you to Kathy Benson.

JIM HASKINS
New York
1977

INTRODUCTION

Like most other blacks, I was pleased when Scott Joplin
was "rediscovered," and I read avidly the books and the
articles about him that began to appear in abundance
even in the mass audience magazines, to say nothing of
the music periodicals. I noticed, however, that the revival
of interest in Joplin was almost exclusively in his music,
that there seemed little in Scott Joplin, the man. What little biographical information was furnished consisted of
paraphrases and rehashes of the few earlier sources that
contained information on Joplin's life, information that
was neither abundant nor in many cases well documented.

I felt that others among the reading public shared my
interest in learning more about Scott Joplin, the man, and
I set out to document the existing information about his
life and, I hoped, to uncover hitherto unknown information, to gain a sense of what it was like to be a black composer at the turn of the century, particularly one with a

mission, as was Joplin. The results of my work are contained in the following pages.

This work has been the most exciting, and the most frustrating, I have ever undertaken. I have made and learned of discoveries that debunk some of the earlier myths about Joplin. I have come extremely close to making other discoveries but have not quite managed to do so. Despite intensive efforts, there are still facts I cannot document. And there is painfully little material relative to Joplin's feelings and thoughts. Too much time has passed, too few family records were kept, too few members of his family survive. What I have done, therefore, is to take the facts I have documented together with the interview material I have gathered and the undocumented legends about Joplin and made what I consider educated conjectures about what is not known. I have provided extensive footnotes, explaining the bases for my conjectures, and I invite the reader to form his or her own opinions.

I feel it is most important to point out here that I had no pre-established opinions and that my interest was not qualified by any political considerations. Now that Joplin has been rediscovered, there are numerous localities that wish to claim importance in his life, a sort of "Scott Joplin slept here" syndrome. Although I am of course deeply grateful to the people who helped me in these various localities, I have made no attempt to fit my interpretations to their desires. I have made no statements that I do not believe.

What has made this project particularly exciting is the continued appearance of new material. Much of the material contained in this book is based on comparatively recent discoveries—a census entry discovered by chance in Shreveport, Louisiana, an old business card found in a secondhand bookstore in Sedalia—and there is every hope that more discoveries of equal importance will be made in the future. Who knows, perhaps someday Joplin's famous lost opera *A Guest of Honor,* will be found in some obscure place, or the trunk full of belongings that Joplin is said to have left in a Baltimore rooming house over fifty years ago will be discovered, or his mother's background will be documented. I welcome such discoveries, for I have never intended this book to constitute the "last word" on the life of Scott Joplin, and I encourage others to utilize this book in the further and hopefully never-ending "search for Scott Joplin."

SCOTT JOPLIN

PROLOGUE

The Rediscovery of Scott Joplin

In April 1917 the family back in Texarkana did not know that Scott Joplin had just died. They learned about it some months afterward, and gradually the news spread to the far-flung cities and towns where other members of the family were scattered. Fred Joplin, Scott's nephew, had disregarded the wishes of his elders and gone on with his piano playing. In 1916, he had left home to pursue his career, but he had not sought out his uncle Scott, if indeed he knew where Scott was living; instead, he had traveled to join friends in Kansas City. At the time of Scott's death he was in Montana, and it was not until some years later, on a return visit to Texarkana, that he learned of his uncle's death.[1]

The Joplins were not a close family. Most of the Joplin men seemed to have traveling in their blood. Scott's brother Robert continued to travel through the Midwest, working as a cook, and giving concerts whenever he could. "I lived in Chicago and he and his wife came to visit me in the early twenties," Fred Joplin recalls. "He

1

was a baritone, and he put on two or three concerts. Now Willie, I never did see him."[2]

Will, another brother of Scott's, had spent some years in St. Louis with Scott and Robert. He had married there, but his wife had died[3] and he had returned to Texarkana for about a year in 1912, taking a room at 411 Hazel Street and listing himself in the city directory as a laborer. He left the town sometime in late 1912 and began to travel again.

Scott's older brother, Monroe, had remained in Texarkana until sometime in early 1912. In 1910 he had listed himself in the city directory as a car cleaner, although he had usually worked as a cook. In 1912 he moved his family to Texarkana's Iron Mountain addition, but shortly thereafter he got a job in Naples, Texas, and went to live there, leaving his family in Texarkana. Rosa, his second wife, became ill, and in 1913 she and her children went to live with a sister in Marshall. She died in 1915 and Monroe remarried. He died in Naples, Texas, in 1933.[4]

Between 1906 and 1913, Scott's father, Jiles Joplin, lived with his granddaughter, Mattie, who had married Reverend Titus Harris and moved over to the Iron Mountain addition. When Rosa and her children went to Marshall, Monroe moved Jiles into their vacated house in the Iron Mountain addition, where the old man lived until he died on September 4, 1922. Monroe, who supplied information for the death certificate, said his father was "100 or more" when he died; actually, Jiles was about eighty.[5]

Eventually, Fred Joplin returned to Texas, where he and his sisters, Mattie Harris, Donita Fowler, and Ethel Brown, maintained the Joplin family ties to the area.[6] But neither they nor other members of Scott Joplin's family, while they were still active, appear to have made much attempt to keep Scott's name alive. Nor did most of Scott's onetime protégés, Scott Hayden, Arthur Marshall, Sam Patterson, and Joseph Lamb among them. Not that any of these people had the influence necessary at that time to bring about a Scott Joplin music festival, or even a Scott Joplin memorial of some sort.

For a time, only Scott's widow, Lottie Joplin, carried the torch. Left alone in New York City, this resourceful woman had continued her boardinghouse business and made it respectable. She remained at 163 West 131st Street, where she had lived with Scott until 1921 and thereafter operated similar establishments at 251 West 131st Street and 212 West 138th Street,[7] housing at various times such music greats as Jelly Roll Morton, Wilbur Sweatman, and Willie "The Lion" Smith. Knowing how important the opera *Treemonisha* had been to her husband, she worked hard to get it produced. "I tried to get it on Broadway for years," she said in 1950, "and I remember that Earl Carroll once seemed really interested in the idea . . . But things never materialize when you want them to, and next I knew, Earl Carroll had gotten into difficulties over some girl and that bathtub of champagne, and he told me, 'Lottie, I guess there's no chance now.'"[8]

Around 1930, Samuel Brunson Campbell, a white pianist whom Scott had befriended during his Sedalia period, took up the cause, stimulated by a rather unusual incident. Years before in Sedalia, Scott had given Campbell a half dollar, dated 1897, and told him to keep it for good luck. Campbell later recalled:

"Well, I carried that half dollar as a good luck piece as Joplin suggested. Then in 1903 I met another pianist in a midwestern city and we became chums. One day we decided to go frog hunting down at the river nearby. We got into a friendly argument as to who was the best shot, so I took my silver half dollar and placed it in a crack on top of a fence post as a target. We measured off and my friend fired and missed. I shot and hit it dead center. The impact of the bullet really put it out of shape, so on our return to the city I went to a blacksmith shop and with a hammer reshaped it as best I could and then carried it as a pocket piece as before. But one day I somehow spent it."

Many years later, Campbell married and moved to California, where he set up a business. On May 1, 1930, a customer paid for a purchase with a silver half dollar—the very same half dollar that Scott Joplin had given him and that Campbell had used as a target twenty-seven years before. Quite naturally, he considered it an omen. It recalled old memories, especially the look in Scott Joplin's eyes as he had presented the coin to Campbell. As Campbell later recalled, "that half dollar seemed to say: 'Why don't you write about Scott Joplin and early ragtime. Write his biography and other articles and sell them to magazines and newspapers?'

"And then it seemed to say: 'Don't you think it would be nice to make a piano recording of his "Maple Leaf Rag" just as he taught you back there in Sedalia, and use the money from these sources to erect a memorial monument over his unmarked grave for what he did in the field of early American music?' I did all that with the exception that I never erected the monument. Instead I sent the money to his widow to help her in an illness of long standing . . . His widow once wrote me, 'Of all Scott's old friends, you are the only one who has ever offered to do anything for him.' It was the least the 'Ragtime Kid' could do for an old friend."[9]

Campbell did indeed write about Joplin, initially in an article called "The Ragtime Kid (An Autobiography)," but it was never published in his lifetime. How hard he tried to get it published is not known, but it is unlikely that it would have inspired much interest. America was in the throes of the Jazz Age. Duke Ellington reigned with his Cotton Club Band. Ragtime seemed dull and mechanical by comparison, and Scott Joplin had been all but forgotten, except by those who had known him or by those few diehard ragtime enthusiasts who quietly set about collecting ragtime memorabilia. Among these enthusiasts was R. J. Carew, who had first heard "Maple Leaf Rag" played by a local music teacher in Gulfport, Mississippi, around 1906, when he was a teen-ager, and who had devoted much of the rest of his life to collecting Joplin rags. Having learned around 1916 that Joplin had written an opera, *Treemonisha*, he made every effort to secure a copy but was unable to do so.

The ragtime underground continued to operate; as if by telepathy, ragtime aficionados learned of each other and sought each other out. In the summer of 1944, a young ragtime enthusiast from Portland, Oregon, Donald E. Fowler, called on Carew to discuss ragtime in general and Joplin's ragtime in particular. The meeting resulted in collaborative articles on Scott Joplin that *The Record Changer* published that year. S. Brunson Campbell saw the articles and contacted Carew. In May and June 1945, *The Record Changer* carried two articles by Campbell/Carew on Joplin's days in Sedalia.

"We were happy to learn that these articles were a

source of some pleasure to Joplin's widow, Mrs. Lottie Joplin, who is still living in New York," wrote Carew in 1946. "Not so long ago the postman left a flat rectangular package inside my screen door. A rather heavy package for its size, I thought, as I tore off the wrappings. With the excess paper out of the way I found myself with a prize in my hands. Yes, it was a copy of Scott Joplin's opera, 'Treemonisha,' autographed by Mrs. Scott Joplin. My thirty-year search for the work had finally ended. S. Brun Campbell wrote me shortly afterward that he had suggested to Mrs. Joplin that she send me a copy of the opera. Needless to say, I am exceedingly grateful to Mrs. Joplin and Mr. Campbell for their kindness in this matter."[10]

Ragtime in general and Scott Joplin's music in particular were beginning to enjoy a renaissance, albeit a minor one, as evidenced by such articles, and about the time they began to appear, Rudi Blesh conceived a book about ragtime and its foremost exponents. With Harriet Janis, Blesh researched the lives of the ragtime greats, and the co-authors were in the enviable position of being able to interview such men as Joseph Lamb and Sam Patterson and Arthur Marshall, for though they were old they were still very much alive and filled with vivid memories of the ragtime era. The resulting book, *They All Played Ragtime,* first published in 1950, brought to the general public for the first time the stories of the early ragtime greats and proved to be the generative work in literature on Scott Joplin. Based to a considerable extent on interviews with Lottie Joplin, the information on Joplin has provided source material for nearly every subsequent work that includes mention of him. The book did not, however, spark a popular Joplin revival.

Interest remained chiefly within the ragtime underground, which began slowly to grow. Here and there across the country pianists began to rediscover ragtime, which led to an appreciation of Joplin's music, which led to curiosity about his background. In April 1959, John Vanderlee, a ragtime pianist in Fort Worth, Texas, and his wife Ann, now deceased, visited Texarkana. Through interviews with the Joplin family and friends and research into city directories and old census records, they compiled the most accurate and detailed account of Joplin's early life up to that time. Their findings were not published, however, until 1973–74, when the *Rag Times* carried their account in two installments.

In 1953 in St. Louis, thirteen-year-old Trebor (Robert spelled backward) Jay Tichenor heard "Maple Leaf Rag" and immediately became a devotee of ragtime and Joplin. He grew up to become a ragtime "professor" himself and the pianist in the saloon of the Goldenrod Showboat, a registered landmark in St. Louis. By 1972 he had amassed countless rags in sheet music form and seven thousand piano rolls, between eight hundred and one thousand of them rags. His Joplin collection is one of the finest in the country and includes a swinging door (he suspects it was to one of the toilets) rescued from the old Rosebud Cafe, where Joplin had played before it was torn down. Proud of Missouri's role in the birth of ragtime and proud that Joplin had spent some years in St. Louis, Tichenor has spent considerable time going through old telephone directories and culling bits of information on Joplin and other black ragtimers in St. Louis from black newspapers of the period.

As time went on the Tichenors and Vanderlees multiplied, and in the late 1960s the underground movement began to surface and coalesce. Dick Zimmerman, a ragtime pianist in California, founded *Rag Times* in May 1966, devoted to the resurgence of the form. Its motto was "Scott Joplin Lives!" and among the articles about ragtime greats, past and present, and current ragtime events, articles on Joplin appear frequently in its pages. The organization that functions as an umbrella for the periodical is called the Maple Leaf Club.

Also in the late 1960s a young musicologist and pianist named Joshua Rifkin, who had previously been interested in ragtime as a precursor of jazz, began to recognize classic ragtime as akin in many respects to classical music. At the time, he was acting as an informal adviser to Nonesuch, a recording company that specialized in Renaissance and Baroque music. He persuaded Nonesuch to issue a recording of Joplin's works. "I felt the music should be treated seriously, that it should be put out on a classical label, with a dignified cover, and literate notes," he says.[11]

Interestingly, some fifty years earlier a writer for the Detroit *News* had urged that ragtime be appreciated by the classicists. "If any musician does not feel in his heart the rhythmic complexities of 'The Robert E. Lee,' I should not trust him to feel in his heart the complexities of Brahms. I cannot understand how a trained musician can overlook its purely technical elements of interest. It has carried the complexities of the rhythmic subdivision of the measure to a point never before reached in the history of music."[12] Unfortunately, both the writer of the article and Scott Joplin were too far ahead of their own time. Joplin had often said that his music would be appreciated only after he had been dead fifty years. He was off by only about three years in his prediction.

The first of three Rifkin recordings of Joplin's work was issued in December 1970 and was an immediate success, not just by classical music recording standards but by music recording standards in general. In the next four years, Nonesuch would issue two more Rifkin recordings of Joplin. Like subsequent recorders of Joplin works, Rifkin played the rags slowly, as Joplin had insisted, giving listeners the opportunity to appreciate the beauties and the intricacies of the works. American musical tastes having changed once again, as is the cyclical tradition of history, American listeners were ready to appreciate them.

At least one segment of American listeners, that is. Reviewing the first Rifkin recording in the Sunday New York *Times* in January 1971, Harold C. Schonberg declared: "Scholars, get busy on Scott Joplin." And among other musicologists, Addison Walker Reed did. His 1973 doctoral thesis at the University of North Carolina, Chapel Hill, included the findings of the Vanderlees and material gathered by the Texarkana Historical Society and Museum. Scott Joplin and his music were still of interest primarily to ragtime enthusiasts and musicologists, however, as pianist and music collector Vera Brodsky Lawrence learned when she tried to find a publisher for a collected edition of Joplin's piano pieces. Twenty-four publishing houses turned her down, feeling the book would not have a sufficiently wide market, before the New York Public Library agreed to do it. Both that first volume of piano pieces and her subsequent collection of Joplin's works for voice have sold exceedingly well. This is not to suggest that the publishers who rejected the idea had poor market-forecasting procedures; they could not foresee that the name Scott Joplin would shortly become a household word and his music as familiar as that of Stevie Wonder.

George Roy Hill, film director, heard a Rifkin recording of Joplin that his oldest son had purchased, and decided the music would make an excellent background for the movie on which he was then working, *The Sting*. Though he was aware that the era of classic ragtime and Joplin's music had preceded the period of the film, which is set in the 1920s, he felt the humor and high spirits of Joplin's rags captured the feeling he wanted. Hill brought in composer Marvin Hamlisch and together they selected the music for the score, which includes "The Entertainer," "Gladiolus Rag," "Pine Apple Rag," "The Ragtime Dance," and "Solace." "The Entertainer" was renamed "The Sting" and served as the title song. Released in 1973, the film *The Sting*, won the Academy Award for Best Picture of the Year in 1974, and the score and title song also won Oscars. By the fall of 1974 the soundtrack of *The Sting* had sold over two million in records and tapes.[18] Suddenly, Joplin's music and Joplin's name were everywhere. By an extremely circuitous route, Scott Joplin had again reached the popular market.

Now, Joplin's rags are available in recordings on a variety of labels by numerous pianists and ensembles. "Maple Leaf Rag," in these recordings, has sold over a million copies. Ragtime pianists proliferate and major ragtime festivals are held each year in cities and towns across the country. The pages of ragtime periodicals are replete with announcements and reports of such gatherings. Rags by many composers are featured, but Scott Joplin seems to hover over these proceedings, never far from rag devotees' minds, his name frequently on their lips.

The towns and cities where Joplin lived at different

times in his life have taken steps to acquaint the world with their role in his career and in his music. In Missouri, particularly in Sedalia and St. Louis, the role of the region in the birth of ragtime was being rediscovered by the mid- to late 1950s. Many Sedalians had not even heard of Scott Joplin until the local newspaper carried an article about him, but once they had learned of him and his connections with Sedalia, they were quick to start a Scott Joplin Memorial Foundation. In 1961 a marble memorial plaque was installed on the corner of Main Street and Lamine Avenue, where the original Maple Leaf Club stood and where a parking lot now operates. It paid tribute not only to Joplin but also to John Stark, his first and most supportive publisher, Arthur Marshall, and Scott Hayden. At first there was talk of exhuming Joplin's body from his grave in New York and bringing it to Sedalia to rest beneath the memorial, but the idea was given up when it was discovered that he was buried in a common grave with two other individuals and it would be difficult to ascertain which one was Scott.[14] In July of 1974, the first Scott Joplin Ragtime Festival was held in Sedalia. The sponsors had hoped to persuade the U. S. Postal Service to issue a Scott Joplin commemorative stamp, but the suggestion was rejected without explanation.

In St. Louis, the building at 2658–60 Delmar Boulevard (formerly Morgan Town Road), Joplin's first residence in the city, was placed on the National Register of Historic Places by the U. S. Department of the Interior in 1977.

About the same time Missourians were beginning to rediscover Joplin, Texarkanans began to learn about their famous former citizen. In 1956, a group of jazz musicians presented a concert to benefit a local church. The master of ceremonies, George Beasley, mentioned Joplin in his

11

introductory remarks and sparked the interest of one of the musicians, Jerry Atkins, a Texarkana businessman. Over the next twenty years, Atkins researched Joplin's Texarkana period, though he found relatively few sources. Through the work of D.A.R. genealogist Mrs. Arthur Jennings and others interested in Texarkana history, a respectable amount of information has been compiled, and in 1971 the Texarkana Historical Society and Museum began to collect in earnest information on Joplin and memorabilia for a special, permanent Joplin exhibit.

In 1973, when the twin cities of Texarkana, Arkansas, and Texarkana, Texas, celebrated their centennial, their most famous citizen was honored with a Scott Joplin Centennial Concert, at which eighty-two-year-old John Vanderlee, who fourteen years earlier had come to town with his wife to gather information on the early life of Scott Joplin, played a selection of the master's rags, and at which Joplin's surviving relatives were honored guests. On November 24, 1975, a bust of Joplin commissioned by the twin city Bicentennial Commission was unveiled at the museum; in December 1975 the Texas side opened the Scott Joplin Park; in March 1976 the Arkansas Historic Preservation Program nominated Orr School for the National Register of Historic Places; in April the Texarkana Museum received a Scott Joplin plaque from the National Federation of Music Clubs; and in 1977 the Texas Historical Commission placed an historical marker on the Texarkana library grounds.

Joplin spent only a brief period of time in Chicago and was listed in the city directory for just one year, but Chicago, too, has paid its tribute. In the late winter of 1975, an elementary school was rededicated as the Scott Joplin Elementary School and the American Society of

Composers, Authors and Publishers unveiled at the ceremony a bronze plaque honoring Joplin.[15]

S. Brunson Campbell would have been pleased with all these tributes and memorials. However, he died in 1952 and so did not live to witness them.

The paucity of information on Joplin's life has moved music collectors and Joplinophiles to search for more, and a number of recent discoveries have helped to fill in the many and sizable gaps in his story. Additions have also been made to the list of Joplin memorabilia. Though Joplin's opera *A Guest of Honor* has yet to be found,[16] one important discovery was made in 1970 by "Piano Roll" Albert Grimaldi. In preparation for a move, Grimaldi was sorting through a group of old piano rolls he had stored in his Los Angeles garage, when he came upon "Silver Swan Rag—Scott Joplin." He had purchased the roll for a quarter from a thrift shop in Los Angeles some fifteen years earlier, when he knew nothing about either Joplin or ragtime. The original titled leader was missing, but Albert had copied the title and composer from the leader onto the roll when he had purchased it. Because the leader was missing and the brand of the roll was unknown, some questioned that the rag was indeed Joplin's. However, subsequently a nickelodeon roll of the rag surfaced in the collection of Don McDonald of Balwin, Missouri, and the rag was found listed in a roll catalogue, credited to Joplin and dated 1914. The roll was transcribed and copyrighted in the name of the Joplin estate, and it was included in *Scott Joplin: Collected Piano Works.*[17]

In 1976 James Fuld of New York found a previously unknown song that Joplin had arranged. "Good-bye Old Gal Good-bye," by H. Carroll Taylor, was published in 1906 by the Foster-Calhoun Company, Evansville, Indiana. Though the sheet music states the song was copy-righted, it was not.[18]

It was inevitable that someone would decide to stage a production of Joplin's opera *Treemonisha,* and in 1972 its world premiere took place at the Atlanta Memorial Arts Center in connection with an Afro-American music work-shop sponsored by Morehouse College. Later in the same year, a second production was presented at Wolf Trap Farm outside Washington, D.C. Both of these early pro-ductions were relatively straightforward renderings based closely not only on Joplin's orchestrations but also on his choreography and staging instructions. Had Scott been alive, both would have "done him proud." But others saw greater potential in *Treemonisha,* the potential for a truly grand production. In May 1975, such a production opened at the Houston Grand Opera. Directed by Frank Corsaro, choreographed by Louis Johnson, and orches-trated by Gunther Schuller, who has recorded several vol-umes of Joplin rags, this production of *Treemonisha* real-ized all of the opera's possibilities, and it received excellent reviews.

Finally in September 1975, Scott Joplin's dream was re-alized. *Treemonisha* opened at the Uris Theater on Broadway and played a limited engagement before packed houses, and though it departed in some ways from Joplin's original concept, it remained true to his basic in-tent. To overcome the inadequacies of the story, Corsaro concentrated on much movement and high-spirited danc-ing and emphasized the whimsy and fantasy in the li-bretto. Franco Colavecchia's costumes and stage sets helped the audience to follow the story, which was at times a difficult task, for Joplin included no spoken dia-logue whatsoever. The producers could have added dia-logue and more material to the plot, but they chose to remain true to the Joplin libretto.

Gunther Schuller was equally loyal to Joplin in the orchestration. "If you want to criticize *Treemonisha* from a cold, academic point of view, you can find plenty of weaknesses," he has said. "For one thing, Joplin had never heard a lot of the music of his day—Stravinsky or Mahler, say—and he used the musical language of the eighteen-forties. But . . . it has a period charm that's indestructible. When I orchestrated it, I resisted the temptation to 'do something' with it. I wrote as closely as possible to what Joplin would have done in terms of the instrumentation and abilities of pit bands of his day. I tried to keep in mind what Joplin would have had in his ear. If I had jazzed it up, it would have killed the period feeling . . . [*Treemonisha*] is a very uneven piece and certainly not a great piece of drama but, on the other side of it, it has some of the most beautiful music Joplin ever wrote."[19]

The theater was small, intimate. The audience had about them an air of expectation, for they realized they were about to witness not just an opera but a bona fide historic event, and as the lights dimmed they leaned forward to register in their memories every moment. At times early in the performance there was an uncomfortable murmur, as they strained to understand the words that were sung and that alone told the story. But as the opera progressed they picked up the unspoken cues that communicated the action—in the expressions in the singers' voices, the fantastical costumes and props, the tremendously expressive dancing. They were no longer constrained to enjoy the show because they wanted so much to see Scott Joplin succeed; they were able to relax and relish it without a sense of obligation. When the curtain came down, they did not want to leave, and when the dancers launched into a second and final rendition of "Aunt Dinah Has Blowed de Horn," the theater fairly rocked with joy. The master would indeed have been pleased. Sadly, Lottie Joplin, who had tried so hard to get *Treemonisha* on Broadway, did not live long enough to witness the triumph. She had died, at the age of seventy-nine, on March 14, 1953.[20]

The production of *Treemonisha* provided the impetus for the awarding to Scott Joplin posthumously of a Pulitzer Prize in 1976. It is probable that the prize was actually awarded to Joplin for the sum of his work and that *Treemonisha* was simply the obvious "hook" on which to hang it. Some critics did not wholeheartedly applaud the award. Gary Giddins, writing in the May 24, 1976, *Village Voice,* stated: "One hesitates to throw a wrench at such a pleasantly ironic, self-congratulatory, but deserving award, except that poor Scott, who died in 1917, is being used as a lever against more considerable black achievement. He has been found worthy because he has been discovered by the conservatory, because his music does not require improvisation, and because he wrote an opera to prove his seriousness."

Many Joplinophiles were not overgratified by the award; for them, the real gratification has been the rediscovery of Joplin by the general public; the enjoyment his music has brought to millions, and their part in helping to make it all happen. But there is a certain pleasure in the knowledge that such vaunted recognition has been given to the man whose common grave remained unmarked for fifty-seven years.

In October 1974 that "oversight" was ameliorated.

ASCAP (American Society of Composers, Authors and Publishers) held a brief service at the site of the fifth grave in the second row of St. Michael's Cemetery in Astoria, Queens. There, on the stubbly patch of ground between two other graves marked by stones, the bronze marker was placed. It read simply "Scott Joplin, American Composer," and gave his birth and death dates. During Joplin's lifetime, most of his fellow composers did not recognize his importance; now, at last, they paid him the honor due him. As the dignitaries stood viewing the marker, a soft breeze came up, wafting across the gravesite brightly colored maple leaves from the large tree nearby.

CHAPTER I

Prelude

In the middle of the nineteenth century, the Republic of Texas was an anomaly, a transition area between the established South and the frontier West. Much of western and northern Texas was wilderness, piney woods and swamplands where Indian tribes lived undisturbed by the scattered squatters and hunters whose connections to civilization were remote and whose allegiance was to themselves alone. East Texas, though more populous, still had about it a wild and woolly frontier flavor. In these days before statehood it was a haven for persons fleeing the laws of neighboring states. But though it lacked civility, it abounded in opportunity, a wide open area, ripe for enterprising men from older, more established regions where the land had already been cleared, the class system installed, a man's opportunities somewhat circumscribed. For the ambitious Southern farmer East Texas was the new frontier, lacking the laws that prevented expansion and the customs that limited unabashed ambition, but in its climate and geography little more than a fresh extension of the South.

The land was rich and fertile, the delightfully mild climate perfect for agriculture. Breezes from the Gulf of Mexico modified the summer heat and produced sufficient and evenly distributed rainfall as well as an active wind movement. Already, cotton was becoming the major cash crop of the region. Areas not cleared for agriculture were richly timbered with pine, oak, hickory, ash, gum, cottonwood, and cypress trees, and the lumber business provided another practically untapped opportunity for the enterprising immigrant. Charles Moores intended to go into farming as well as the lumber business when at the age of sixty-two he left the area near Longtown, Fairfield County, South Carolina, with his sons Eli, twenty-three, and Reuben, twenty-one, to purchase land and establish a homestead for his family. They arrived in East Texas in February 1838 and acquired the John Jackson and Howard Ethridge and part of the E. T. Jackson headright surveys in the area now known as Red Springs in Bowie County.[1] It was wooded, fertile land with abundant water. Several streams as well as Barr's Creek would provide water for the home and mill they intended to build, and Trammels Trace[2] was already an established main road for the post office and small store planned for the village that would be called Mooresville. They built a house, purchased one or two slaves, and about a year and a half later Charles Moores returned to South Carolina for the rest of the family. During his absence, Eli and Reuben cleared the land intended for cultivation and built additional living quarters.

Charles Moores, his wife Mary Harrison Moores, and their children, including sons Thomas, twenty, and Anderson, eighteen, set out for Texas in February 1840, leading a sizable entourage of other families, livestock, and slaves. A daughter, Nancy, age thirty, and her husband James Rochelle, remained in South Carolina, where they owned slaves and operated a farm of their own. The Moores party traveled by oxcart, wagon train, and carriage during their more than three-month journey. During a stop at Bell Buckle, Tennessee, Thomas Moores met and married Sarah Norvell, who joined the group as they continued westward. They arrived at their new home on May 24, 1840.[3]

The Moores house fronted on a lake and was built of logs hand-hewn to resemble clapboards. The kitchen and smokehouse were separate buildings and a slave quarter was erected some yards behind the house. After the rest of the family and their fellow travelers arrived, Mooresville took shape quickly. It was officially recognized as a postal depot in 1841, and Reuben Moores served as the first postmaster. Immediately upon her arrival, Mary Harrison Moores asked that a church be erected, which she named Harrison Chapel in memory of her parents. Similar in appearance to the Moores house, it had glass windows and a balcony reserved for slaves. After it was destroyed by fire, in 1842 another church was organized at Mooresville by Methodist circuit rider J. W. P. McKenzel.

By the time of the 1846–48 Mexican War over Texas, which was admitted to the Union in 1845, Mooresville had become a village of sorts. Major J. P. Gaines, whose cavalry regiment from Kentucky camped at Mooresville, wrote in his diary, "Marched 20 miles from Red River to Moores, ticks innumerable, a good plantation, and a wealthy man, store, grog shop . . . Bought an old-fashioned splint bottom chair for which I paid one dollar."[4] By 1848 Charles Moores owned 6,625 acres of land which stretched toward the Sulphur River, where Moores Landing adjoined the James Giles headright in Cass County. He was wealthy, as Major Gaines had noted, and though it is likely that he would have returned to South Carolina to get his daughter's children and property under any circumstances, his wealth made it considerably easier for him to do so.

Nancy Moores Rochelle had died in February 1843. Her husband, James, died early in 1850, leaving not only four sons and a daughter but slaves and other property as well. Shortly after receiving word of James Rochelle's death, Charles Moores left Texas for South Carolina to get the Rochelle children and property. He arrived back in Texas with his charges in late August 1850.[5] The grandchildren, John, Charles, Henry, Eugene, and Mary, were welcomed by the large, extended family that comprised Mooresville, a family related both by blood ties and by their common ties to the land on which they had settled just a decade before. The slaves, too, were welcomed by their fellow slaves, who took particular care to make the new children feel welcome, for they were unused to the strange country so many hundreds of miles away from home. One of these new slave children was named Jiles.[6] A small boy of medium dark color, Jiles was shortly to be accorded a type of respect to which slaves in Texas, or in any other slave state for that matter, were rarely privileged. In September 1850 his name would be recorded in a census.

Just a few weeks after Charles Moores's return, Mooresville was visited by a census taker, whose duty was to record the number of slaves in Bowie County. Under the

"Three-Fifths Compromise," slave states were accorded representation for three-fifths of their slave population in addition to that for their white population. Thus, every ten years a slave census was taken in all the counties of the slave states. The purpose of the slave census, unlike that of the federal census, was to record numbers, ages, and sexes, not names. There was not even a blank on the census form for the slaves' names, and yet in that year Bowie County census taker Benjamin Booth did record the names of slaves. This is what he listed under the name Chas. Moores:

	AGE	SEX	COLOR
Tillie	20	F	B
John Lott	16	M	"
Nelly	30	F	"
Dove	11	F	"
Jiles	6	M	"
Synthia	5	F	"
May (or Mary)	(illegible)	(illegible)	(illegible)[7]

Charles Moores had not been back in Mooresville long before he was visited by Benjamin Booth, and undoubtedly he was surprised by Booth's request for the names of his slaves. He had little trouble remembering their names, for he had only a few, but their ages were more difficult to ascertain, particularly those of the slaves newly brought from South Carolina. When asked Jiles's age, he thought for a moment, considered the boy's small stature, and gave his age as six. Actually, Jiles was probably about eight.[8]

By the time young Jiles arrived in East Texas, that area had acquired considerable stability and homogeneity of population. Although there was a constant influx of people, they were primarily from the older Southern states, especially Alabama and the other states along the Gulf of Mexico. These people had brought their customs with them, and by 1850, East Texas was simply a younger version of the South, its economic and social systems those of the established Southern states. Slaves were an integral part of these systems and comprised more than a third of the state's population. In Bowie County, according to the 1850 census, there were 1,641 slaves. In some counties in eastern and southeastern Texas the slave population was larger than that of whites. (By 1860 the 182,566 slaves would constitute 50 per cent of the state's population.) Relationships between masters and slaves were as varied as in the other slave states, ranging from benign paternalism to primitive inhumanism. Relations between masters and slaves in Mooresville were of the paternalistic sort, for the slave inhabitants were few, young and chiefly female. Mary Harrison Moores had early provided for the slaves' religious instruction by ordering a gallery for them in her church. Undoubtedly she insisted on a similar area for slave worship in the new church that was built after the Harrison Chapel was destroyed by fire. The Rochelle slaves were especially well treated, for they and their offspring would become the property of the Rochelle children when they came of age. Charles Moores held them in trust for his grandchildren until he died in 1852, whereupon trusteeship of these slaves passed to other family members until the grandchildren reached their majority.[9]

Jiles grew up in relative comfort. When he arrived at Mooresville, he was too young to work in the fields, and he was assigned chores in and around the house. There

24

was much to do to keep up the Moores home-place. It was a frequent gathering spot for neighbors in the surrounding area, among them the families of Elliott, Whitaker, Jarrett, and Hooks. Extra rooms above the main hall were kept especially for circuit preachers, itinerant peddlers, and other travelers. Often the large hall hosted dances, the steps leading to the upper rooms conveniently serving as a box for the string band on such occasions. When he was young, Jiles acted as a serving boy to the guests, watching with fascination as the dancers tripped through their complex square dance routines and polka-like schottisches while the musicians played. Even an experienced observer here would be hard put to differentiate the music and dancing from those of established South Carolina society. This was especially true of the music. Almost entirely European in character, it had undergone no more change in its transplantation from South Carolina to Texas than it had from Europe to America. Jiles showed an aptitude for this music, and particularly for the violin, and when he was old enough he became part of the plantation's string band, standing on the stairs leading up from the main hall and playing for the colorfully dressed dancers below.[10]

Mooresville was not very different from any small Southern plantation area, although there was far greater opportunity for land expansion, and the slave population grew accordingly. By the mid-1850s, however, considerable differences could be seen, for East Texas, unlike the other slave regions to the east, did not feel many of the tensions that resulted from the heightened hostility between North and South that was to lead to the formation of the Confederacy and the outbreak of the Civil War. Mooresville prospered. As children married, they were given tracts of land on which they built homes of their own and which they worked for income to buy more land. In 1847, when Eli Moores had married, Charles Moores had deeded 166 acres of the Howard Ethridge headright survey to his son, an area that would later become part of Texarkana, Texas.

A few miles away from Mooresville, the village of Hooks was enjoying a similar period of rapid growth. Warren and Elizabeth Roberts Hooks had come to East Texas from North Carolina by way of Alabama.[11] Like Charles Moores, Warren Hooks had gone west searching for land and greater opportunity, had cleared acres of land for farming and built a sawmill, purchased slaves,[12] and expanded his family holdings through his children. Hooks children and grandchildren intermarried with Moores and Rochelle children and grandchildren, and the families exchanged gifts and entered into business dealings with each other. Probably sometime in the late 1850s the Mooreses' slave Jiles left Mooresville and became part of the household of Warren Hooks, perhaps as a wedding gift to Warren's daughter, Minerva. Minerva married a man named Josiah Joplin, and it was this man's last name that Jiles took as his own.[13]

Jiles did not stay long in the Hooks household. Although it is not known when or under what circumstances, Jiles was freed when he was in his late teens, several years before the Emancipation Proclamation was issued in Texas.[14] He could probably have remained in the relatively benign atmosphere of Hooks and Mooresville, but he chose instead to travel south, perhaps intending to make his way to one of the large cities. Near the area around present-day Linden he met Florence Givins, and he changed his mind.

Florence Givins had been freeborn in Kentucky[15] in 1841 and had traveled with her father, Milton, and her grandmother, Susan, to Texas, where the family served in the capacity of slave overseers for white farmers.[16] Florence was a comely young woman, a year older than Jiles and sufficiently shorter in height to bolster the ego of this man who is said to have been very short. Though she might have preferred a husband who had been born free, as she had been, such men were scarce in rural Texas, and at least Jiles was a freedman. At the ages of about eighteen and nineteen respectively, Jiles Joplin and Florence Givins entered into the only marriage-like arrangement available to most blacks, slave or free, at that time. As Zenobia Campbell, who knew the Joplins in Texarkana, once said, "Back then, colored people didn't pay much attention to marriage and divorce. When they married, they just jumped over the broomstick."[17] Their first child, Monroe, was born just as the Civil War was breaking out.[18]

With Arkansas, Texas seceded from the Union in 1861. During the war Marshall, Texas, became the Confederate capital-in-exile of Missouri, and North Texas became an important area for Missouri slaveowners. But Texas was never a major campaign front, and while it felt some economic effects from the war that raged to the east of it— closed ports and trails and the halting of railroad construction—it was not blanketed by the propaganda that accompanied the slavery question in the states to the east. For the most part, slaves in East Texas hardly knew their freedom was at issue.

The Joplins lived as they had prior to the war, working in the fields, living day to day with little hope for the future and little understanding of the war's implications for their lives. Nor were whites in East Texas particularly affected. The cotton plantations and timber businesses continued production, and though shipping was circumscribed the planters and millowners did not suffer inordinately. Both products could be stored for long periods of time while waiting for a mule-drawn wagon to take them to Jefferson, Texas, or for a riverboat to get through a federal blockade or arrive by a more circuitous route; and since these steamboats with their wide, flat guards, had a capacity of from one thousand to two thousand bales of cotton they could frequently accommodate a large portion of the region's crop. Although the arrival of a steamboat in the towns along the rivers was always an occasion, during the war years it was especially so. When a boat arrived during the day, nearby slaves were allowed to interrupt their work to go down to the dock and witness its landing. At night, the slaves lit pine knot torches to facilitate the docking, the excitement of the event heightened by the flickering lights. The arrival of a steamboat was a welcome interruption in the monotony of their lives.

On June 19, 1865, the Emancipation Proclamation was issued at Galveston. It came as no surprise to most Texans, for the so-called irresistible conflict between the states had been effectively over for some time. Still, whites in the slave counties of Texas worried about the effects of Emancipation. While they had expected it to come, they had hoped for a more gradual process, and if such a sudden change in the slaves' status must occur they questioned why its official announcement had to be made so close to harvesttime.

Across the South it was a time of social and economic upheaval. The Civil War had rent the nation, tearing North and South apart. The Confederate states were economically devastated. Yet, these same states were expected somehow to provide economic and other opportunities for the freedmen within their borders, freedmen unprepared for freedom. Clearly the states neither could nor intended to provide adequately for the former slaves, and for their part, many of the former slaves did not care to remain in the South anyhow. Theoretically, the mid- and late 1860s were the first time that they were able to move about freely. The North could not absorb all who wanted to leave the South; the West seemed large enough to accommodate all comers and it conjured up magical images in the minds of blacks just as it did in those of whites.

So they traveled westward, doing their best to avoid the bands of white men that patrolled the country roads to drive back wandering blacks, not to look at the bodies of murdered Negroes who were frequently found on or near the highways and roads, to escape the reign of terror that prevailed in many regions of the South. Some who made it to the Texas border managed to continue on, to the frontier areas where they acquired land or became cowboys or soldiers working for the federal government, which had assumed responsibility for frontier defense in Texas. Others stalled somewhere en route. They needed money, contracted to work on farms along the way, and after a couple of years lost the sense of idealism that would have kept them going. Or, they chose to remain in the more prosperous and more liberal population centers, taking the menial jobs that were available to them.

The newly freed slaves of eastern and southeastern Texas were even less prepared for freedom than their counterparts in the Southern states. Slaves in Arkansas, Louisiana, and Georgia, for example, had seen tangible evidence of the fight to make them free. In those areas where federal troops had moved in, the slave population had even gained some freedoms before the end of the war and had thus been given the opportunity to "try out" freedom before it was formally conveyed. Most slaves in Texas had been far removed from the war and cut off from much of its propaganda. On being informed that they were now free, many had so little comprehension of the concept that their lives remained relatively unaffected. Others misapprehended the role of the federal government, believing that if it had set them free then it would also provide for them materially. During the summer and fall of 1865 white farmers anxiously tried to contract with their former slaves as paid laborers or sharecroppers, but often with little success. A Wharton County planter named Green C. Duncan complained that "the negroes still wont [sic] hire—want to wait until Christmas."[19] Many of the freedmen believed that at Christmas the Government would confiscate their former masters' lands and redistribute them among the newly freed slaves.

Christmas passed, and no such steps to make economic provision for the freedmen occurred. After brief, brave forays away from the plantations, most returned to their former masters, defeated by the irony of a policy dictated by the North and resisted by the South. Eventually they entered into labor contracts with white farmers. However, during the year 1865–66 there was sufficient migration of freedmen to constitute a social and agricultural problem.

Jiles and Florence were probably not among these migrants. It is likely that they remained in the vicinity of what is now Linden, near Florence's father and grandmother. They were in familiar surroundings and chose to remain there rather than risk the unknown. Besides, they had a small son to raise, and traveling around the country was no condition under which to raise a child. They signed on as laborers with William and Elizabeth Caves at Caves Springs, as had Susan and Milton Givins.[20]

Two other families of black freedmen were living on the Caves property, the Crows and the Shepherds. Though theoretically free and under labor contracts with the Caveses, these three black families, like those in other former slave counties of Texas, were hardly more than slaves. Forced to purchase their essentials from the Caveses and to give them a percentage of their crop, they were left with little to show for a year's work.

There were certain differences between their former and present statuses, however. With Emancipation and Presidential Reconstruction in 1865, a constitutional convention had been convened in Texas. The new constitution provided for more civil rights for the freedmen than did the new constitution of any of the other former members of the Confederacy. Freedmen, though denied the franchise, were legally able to own property, enter into contracts, and seek recourse in the courts for alleged wrongs done to them. On August 20, 1866, President Johnson had declared Texas reconstructed and readmitted to the Union. But most Texans were unwilling to accept the liberal provisions contained in the new state constitution. By the time of the President's declaration, the constitution had already begun to be eroded by a series of "black codes" passed by the legislature. While their wording did not specifically mention the freedmen, their provisions were clearly aimed at them and at restoring the stability of the labor market. Laws regulating apprenticeships, vagrancy, and labor contracts, combined with proscriptions against intermarriage, holding public office, suffrage, serving on juries, and testifying in cases in which blacks were not involved, effectively reduced the status of the freedmen to second-class citizenship at best.

With the passage of the harsher Congressional Reconstruction acts, the social and political status of the freedmen would change once more. The first of these acts became law on March 2, 1867, whereupon Texas was declared unreconstructed and placed under provisional government once again. A new constitutional convention was convened in 1868, the year Scott Joplin was born.

Scott, the second son of Jiles and Florence Joplin, was born on November 24 of that year, although no record of his birth has ever been found.[21] In most Southern and Western states at that time the birth of a black infant was not considered sufficiently noteworthy to be officially recorded. During slavery, records of births and deaths of slaves, although they were not usually listed by name, were kept by slave masters, much as they recorded the acquisition or loss of other property. After Emancipation, few such records were kept. Federal censuses continued, however, and after Emancipation they included names and ages of freedmen and their families. In 1975, Charles Steger of Longview, Texas, was researching old Cass County families in Shreveport, Louisiana, municipal archives when he came upon a previously undiscovered Joplin entry. In the 1870 census, under the name of Caves were listed Jiles Joplin, Florence, Monroe, and Scott, age 2. It is an extremely important "find," for it is the earliest known record of Scott Joplin's existence.[22]

Theoretically the milieu into which Scott was born was a hopeful one for blacks in Texas, although it is unlikely that his parents were very much aware of the new laws

affecting him. The 1868 constitutional convention had
drawn up a new document, the Constitution of 1869, that
granted more rights to Negroes, notably suffrage and an
equal share in the distribution of money appropriated for
public schools. But the convention had been marred by
extreme factionalism between representatives from the
western portions of the state, where there were few black
inhabitants, and those from the eastern sections, where
there were many. In fact, some delegates from western
Texas favored division of the state and creation of a new
state from the areas inhabited by large numbers of blacks.
Nothing came of the proposal, and the new constitution
was adopted, but it was not generally adhered to in the
eastern regions of the state. While more well established
than western Texas, eastern Texas was still relatively
young. Disputes were frequently settled by means of
arms, and the rudimentary legal system had little power.
When whites were brought to trial, juries were generally
very lenient, particularly when a case involved the killing
or injuring of a black. On the other hand, juries were very
strict in dispensing "justice" when a black was accused of
assaulting a white. Blacks needed very little coaching on
how to behave when they were around whites. After all,
they'd had years of practice before Emancipation.

White backlash was considerable. In the first eight
months of the year Scott was born there were 379 murders
of freedmen by whites (ten of whites by Negroes) in
Texas. Despite the constitutional guarantee of schooling
for blacks, in the outlying areas opposition to such schools
was so great as to be almost prohibitive.[23] What few
schools there were in these areas were frequently at-
tacked; some were burned, and the teachers whipped,

beaten, and otherwise persecuted. It was considered the lowest condition for a white to be a teacher of blacks.

In the larger population centers, and in cities like Houston and Galveston, where the Freedmen's Bureau made strong inroads, blacks were enjoying a period of opportunity, wherein they were able to exercise their civil rights, elect black officeholders, and enjoy some of the fruits of political influence. But for the most part the blacks who reaped the greatest benefit during that period simply parlayed their influence while Texas was under federal supervision. For blacks in the outlying areas, the liberal provisions of the Reconstruction constitution only made life more complicated and gave whites more reason to resent them. They dared not try to exercise their rights, for they had no Freedmen's Bureau to support and protect them. Typical descriptions of such outlying districts from the *Texas Almanac* of 1867: Nacogdoches County— "Negroes work tolerably well, without a Bureau; their behavior is very good . . ."; Jasper County—"the Negroes behave very well . . . They are very contented as there have been no Freedmen's Bureau or Federal troops, white or black, to make them otherwise."

Back in 1865, noted black abolitionist Frederick Douglass had optimistically declared: "Everybody has asked, 'What shall we do with the Negro?' I have but one answer. Do nothing with us! If the apples will not remain on the tree of their own strength, let them fall! I am not for tying them on the tree in any way. And if the Negro cannot stand on his own legs, let him fall also. All I ask is, give him a chance. If you see him on his way to school, let him alone. If you see him going to the dinner-table at a hotel, let him go! If you see him going to the ballot-box, don't disturb him. If you see him going into a workshop, just let him alone. If you will only untie his hands and give him a chance, I think he will live. He will work as readily for himself as the white man."[24]

But blacks were not given the opportunity to work for themselves, nor were they let alone. After Texas was admitted to the Union for the second and last time in 1870, the Freedmen's Bureau left the state, and blacks were left on their own, economically weak scapegoats, symbols of what the war had cost, symbols of what white former slaveowners had lost. Like so many other black families, the Joplins had settled into a condition of semislavery, one that differed little from slavery times except that it was in some ways less secure. They lived on and worked another man's land in exchange for a roof over their heads and food for the growing number of mouths in the household; one year after Scott, the Joplins' third son, Robert, was born. They were restless, looking for greater opportunity. They moved farther south, settling for a time near the town of Jefferson[25] until the chance for railroad work caused Jiles to take his family to Texarkana.[26]

CHAPTER II

Texarkana

Prior to the war there had been little serious railroad-building activity in the Southwest. Most of the important cotton-producing areas were near rivers, and steamboats, which connected North and South through the great river systems, were deemed sufficient for the area's needs. During the Mexican War, the federal government had considered supporting a southern transcontinental railway system to carry supplies to the troops stationed along the Californian and Mexican frontiers. Others, in and out of government, had begun to recognize the need for a transcontinental railway system of some sort, although there was debate over which areas the line should pass through. Stephen Douglas, chairman of the Senate Committee on Territories, suggested in Congress that the line should be built through the northern states. Jefferson Davis of Mississippi, then Secretary of War, had considered and indeed had conducted experiments with camels to solve the problems of east-west transportation through the Southwest. He suggested connecting such camel trails with a railroad system to be built from Memphis, Tennessee, or Vicksburg, Mississippi to El Paso, Texas, and through his influence legislation was passed under which builders of such a railroad would be entitled to every other section of land through which the railroad passed, providing that such land was not already owned or inhabited. At the same time, New Orleans businessmen were supporting the idea of a railroad that would extend around the Gulf through the present New Mexico and end at a point on the Pacific Coast.

While talk of such possibilities continued, some railroad companies began tentative steps toward the realization of a southern transcontinental system. In 1851 the St. Louis & Iron Mountain Railroad Company was incorporated by an act of the Missouri legislature and established to build a railroad from St. Louis to Pilot Knob, Missouri. Two years later, the Arkansas legislature approved the incorporation of the Cairo & Fulton Railroad Company, whose purpose was to construct a line from Cairo, Illinois, to Fulton, Arkansas, a town situated on the Red River near the Texas border. The Civil War and several major floods interrupted the work of these two railroad companies until 1870, when the St. Louis & Iron Mountain Railroad established and incorporated an Arkansas division for the purpose of extending the line from Pilot Knob to the Arkansas border, where it would join with the Cairo & Fulton road.

In March 1871, the Texas & Pacific Railway Company was established by an act of Congress, the only line operated under federal charter. Its purpose was to build a road from Dallas that would connect with the Cairo & Fulton road, which intended to extend its line to some major point in the Southwest. Initially, the directors of the Cairo & Fulton had planned to carry their road along the north bank of the Red River from Fulton to Shreveport, Louisiana, but the leading citizens of Shreveport objected to the planned route, fearing that it would compete with and hamper the city's established and prosperous river transportation business.[1] Officials of the two railroads then met and decided to connect up at Nash, Texas, a town just over the Arkansas-Texas border in the extreme northeast corner of the state. This plan, too, proved unworkable, for the Cairo & Fulton was unable to obtain a charter from Texas. The officials met again and decided this time to tie up at a point due north of Shreveport amid the pine forests at the junction of the Texas and Arkansas borders. Located on a high sandy ridge ten miles west of Red River and ten miles east of Sulphur River, thirty miles north of the Louisiana line, this site was traversed by what had come to be known as the Great Southwest Trail, for hundreds of years the main trunk line of travel from the Indian villages of the Mississippi River country to those of the South and West. It was also strategically located between the city of St. Louis and the commercial centers of Louisiana. It was the area that would become, officially, Texarkana.

Probably this nebulous region was already known unofficially as Texarkana, a name invented to settle confusion, or perhaps to acknowledge the confusion, about the population center that developed there. From a basis of four families in 1864 two scattered settlements had gradually grown up at this site, one in Bowie County, Texas, and one in Lafayette (soon to be Miller) County, Arkansas.

The name *Texarkana* had been coined before the Civil War, although it had not necessarily been applied to this area. It was the name of a steamboat, one of the twelve that made regular runs on the Red River between Shreveport and Fulton until it sank on August 31, 1870. And according to legend, a man named Swindle, who operated a small grocery store at Red Land in Bossier Parish, Louisiana, manufactured and sold for many years a concoction called "Texarkana Bitters." Back in 1849 a Dr. Josiah Fort had erected a sign bearing the name on his property after learning that a railroad, which owned adjoining land, had plans for the area. The most directly traceable originator of the official name, however, is Colonel Gus Knobel, a surveyor for the Cairo & Fulton Railroad.

Knobel was ordered to survey and mark the site agreed upon by the Cairo & Fulton and Texas & Pacific directors, and when he had chosen a location for the two roads to connect, he took a pine board, wrote three letters for Texas, three letters for Arkansas, and three for Louisiana and nailed it to a tree nearby. "TEX-ARK-ANA," he is reported to have said. "This is the name of the town that is to be built here."[2] The two railroad companies proceeded to buy up land in the area, and the first addition of Texarkana was obtained from Eli Moores. The Carsner headright survey, which he had purchased back in 1849–50 for a wagon and a team of oxen, had long been in dispute, and when a speculator filed and paid the Carsner heirs $578 for unlocated land, Moores deeded his interest in the property to the Texas & Pacific Railway, although ownership of the land continued to be a matter of dispute.[3]

Work by the two railroads began shortly after Colonel Gus Knobel completed his survey, the Texas & Pacific laying its tracks north from Dallas via Nash and the Cairo & Fulton proceeding west from Fulton. With each thud of the mauls on the spikes, with each new section of rail that was laid, Texarkana came a bit more into being. The area experienced a large influx of people—land speculators, clever entrepreneurs, shysters, representatives of every segment of white society. Men found work with the railroads, women arrived in search of husbands or to work in the saloons and gambling houses that were hastily erected to serve the needs and take the money of the railroad men. The sound of nails being pounded into boards was ubiquitous as frame buildings were quickly erected on newly cleared sites. Blacks came, too, for there was little racial discrimination in railroad hiring practices. Although most were employed as common laborers, some were track layers, menders, brakemen, engineers, and mechanics. Jiles Joplin obtained work as a common laborer.[4]

As the standard gauge Texas & Pacific train approached Texarkana, the air for miles around was electric with excitement. The target date for completion of the Texas & Pacific tracks to the Texas border was December 7, 1873. Scott Joplin was five years old, old enough to share in the expectation and jubilation. The small town of Texarkana, Texas, stood proudly, rising up out of the lush surrounding forests. Stumps of varying heights dotted the main streets, and numerous mudholes made travel through the town an adventure for all but the most seasoned visitors. People from outlying districts began to arrive days in advance, in wagons and buggies and on horseback, and by the morning of December 7 the small town was bulging with people camped on the streets and in the surrounding forests. It was a time when the community was united in its pride and jubilation, when blacks were almost included in the general festivities at the site where the iron horse would enter the town. Small boys ran to the tracks and put their ears to the ground, listening for the approaching train, and when the unmistakable rumbling sound could be heard men mounted their horses and galloped off to meet it. At four o'clock that afternoon the huge black engine roared into view, embers flying from its smokestack and black smoke practically obscuring its form. The train screeched to a halt. The band took up its welcoming tune, and the crowd cheered the debarking railroad officials who had come to preside over the ceremony. But the wildest applause was reserved for the train operators. Grimy-faced, wearing their cloth caps and thick cloth gloves, they were the real heroes. Not one young boy in the crowd did not want to be just like them, and they were joined in these sentiments by a considerable number of grown men.

On December 8, 1873, the day after the arrival of the Texas & Pacific train, Major H. L. Montrose, an agent of the railroad who had arrived on that train, set up business on a wide tree stump in the middle of Broad Street. Texarkana, Texas, was up for sale. The town had been divided into lots, and some forty persons were on hand to buy them, those who already lived on the lots being given first option. Among the first purchasers was Eli Moores, and soon families from Mooresville began moving to Texarkana.[5] No blacks in the area could afford to buy these lots, which, for residential purposes sold for $200–$250.[6]

With the division of the Texas side of town into lots, a rudimentary system of streets, little more than bypaths, was established, the streets given names like Olive and Pine and Spruce and Maple in consideration of the various types of trees that abounded in the area. This practice was continued on the Arkansas side after it was divided

into lots and put up for sale in January of 1874 with the
arrival of the Cairo & Fulton Railroad.

Texarkana was to see more railroad construction in en-
suing years and a corresponding influx of both whites and
blacks who brought the population to 2,500 by the time
the town was one year old. Initially, the blacks tended to
cluster on the Arkansas side, in an area of rolling hills
called Near-Town on the northern edge of the settlement.
But a small black section developed across the state line
in Texas as well, and it is here, probably on Pine Street off
State Line Avenue, that Jiles Joplin rented a small frame
house for his family,[7] which numbered six by 1875. (A
daughter, Osie, had been born in 1870.[8]) The area was a
black "quarter" dotted with shotgun shacks rented out by
white landlords, but it did not contrast starkly with the
rest of Texarkana. All of the buildings were of frame construction. It was a lusty frontier town replete with saloons, gamblers, and gunmen. There was much land yet
to be cleared, and wild game such as deer, wild turkey,
and prairie chickens abounded in the forests a short dis-
tance away. Wagons and oxteams were almost the sole
means of transportation other than horses, and a man had
to be quite wealthy to own an oxteam.

For young Scott Joplin, Texarkana was an exciting
place to be. The sandy hills and spring mudholes presented numerous opportunities for play, and the town was
abustle with continual activity. Here land was being
cleared, there new frame houses were being erected,
often to replace earlier structures that had been destroyed
by fire. Tinderbox-like, the town buildings frequently
burned, and it was exciting to watch the townspeople
form bucket brigades and pass buckets of water to throw
on the fire. Perhaps, like most young boys, Scott also

looked forward to being part of the bucket brigade, as his
father frequently was.[9] The streets were being cleared of
stumps by men who satisfied their county tax obligations
in doing so. Caravans of cattle moved along the roads on
their way to the railroads to the east. Wild ducks were
brought in by the wagonload and sold for five cents a
head; flocks of wild turkeys were driven through the
streets on their way to area markets and these, too, could
be purchased. And there were always new people, a constant influx of new people.

Some were freedmen, come to Texas to work on the
railroads, or to Texarkana to work in the first sawmill,
built around 1874. The majority of the new immigrants
who arrived in or passed through Texarkana, however,
were whites who had left the older Southern states of Alabama, Georgia, Mississippi, and the Carolinas where
there was little opportunity for them, lured by the promise of cheap land and a chance for a new start. A few
were well-to-do, but according to one observer the majority were a "dense crowd of poor forlorn, wasted ill-clad
people . . . They are going to Texas for new homes but
with scant means."[10]

The waves of immigrants boded ill for the situation of
the Texas freedmen. Their most visible impact was political, and by the early 1870s the influence of the Republican Party in Texas had been reduced drastically. A new
constitutional convention was held in 1875, and attempts
to restrict Negro suffrage by levying a poll tax, though
defeated, revealed the declining political influence of
black Texans and their Republican allies. Provisions for
an elective judiciary and apportionment of districts
caused those counties with 30 to 70 per cent black popu-

lation to be gerrymandered so as to give whites control in the election of judges.

Harder to measure but also devastating to the Texas freedmen were the antiblack sentiments of these new immigrants. Most grudgingly acceded to the Negro's right to personal freedom and to own property, but attempts to grant him social equality met stubborn and sometimes fierce resistance.[11] The 1870s witnessed a gradual decline in Texas legislative provisions for social equality for the freedmen. While they continued to have suffrage, there was growing sentiment in favor of restricting it in various ways. Education laws and provisions were also excellent indicators of the state's attitudes toward black social equality.

Although Texas ranked above the other Southern states in providing education for blacks during the three decades following the war, it did far better in educating its white population. The whole question of education during the Reconstruction era was a complex one, for it involved a shift from a haphazard system of private schools to a system of free public education supported by tax dollars. And if there was considerable initial resistance on the part of whites to paying for the education of other (white) men's children, then it can well be imagined how fierce was the resistance to educating the freedmen and their children.

The Freedmen's Bureau had taken the first steps toward establishing schools for blacks during the years immediately following the war, but because of white hostility these schools were located primarily in the Houston and Galveston areas. By the time the Freedmen's Bureau ended its work in 1870, the state had made provisions for at least a rudimentary public school system. The Constitution of 1869, framed by a Republican-dominated convention, provided for a system of public schools for all children ages six to eighteen and for compulsory attendance four months each year. However, in 1872 the Democrats gained control of the legislature and the educational provisions of the Constitution of 1869 were not enforced. In the early 1870s five Negro schools in East Texas were burned, and a number of cases of whipping and persecution of white teachers in Negro schools were reported.

In the early days of Texarkana there were no schools, either for whites or blacks. By 1875 the formerly state-run public education system had been decentralized and a community system established, which allowed whites in many outlying areas to disregard education for their own as well as for black children. Texarkana was one such community. But at least some of the Joplin children were being educated in a fashion, through private tutoring, for their parents were anxious that they learn to read and write.[12] Next to land, education was regarded by the freedmen as the most important ingredient of success. After the first public school system was established in Texas in 1871, blacks were so enthusiastic that the colored schools were overflowing. When it was not possible to lease a building, Negroes offered their churches, and often put up school buildings with their own funds.[13] In Texarkana, as in other small towns, children were taught by members of the black community who could read and write and who were paid with food by their pupils' parents.[14]

At the same time, the Joplin children were learning about music. Both Jiles and Florence were musically inclined and talented. Jiles was a violinist and Florence played the banjo and sang.[15] Both parents encouraged musical interest in their children, for music was the life-blood of Southern blacks, the safest and most profound medium for expression of their feelings. In black Texarkana, music was as integral a part of life as breathing. Indeed, it might be considered one reason why black people in the 1870s were breathing at all.

Music had contributed significantly to black survival during slavery. When the slaves were brought to the New World from Africa, a common practice among slave masters was to avert possible revolts by grouping together slaves from different tribes, speaking different dialects. In order to communicate with each other verbally, it was necessary for the slaves to learn the pidgin English their owners used when speaking to them and to speak to each other in that dialect.

For a time, they communicated with each other by means of drums which they fashioned from wood and whatever other materials were available. But when white owners discovered the slaves were using the drums to send messages from plantation to plantation, they were outlawed. The slaves then circumvented the laws by devising ways to re-create drum sounds, most notably by tapping their heels in a particular way on a wooden floor. Even after drums were allowed once more, heel-tapping and handclapping remained an integral part of plantation slave music.[16]

For centuries music was the slaves' only effective means of communication, and the highly developed African rhythmic system allowed for considerably greater and more subtle mood variations than Western European systems. For the slave, rhythm could create as well as resolve tension, and tonal variation could encourage an individualism otherwise denied to the slaves—the individualism of the single person as well as that of the group. The nature of the slaves' work precluded expressive use of the hands and feet, for they were engaged in rapidly moving along the rows of cotton and picking the cotton bolls or swinging pickaxes on the roads, or unloading cargo on the docks. The voice, however, was free, and the slaves sang constantly as they worked, particuarly songs employing a call-mass response form.

> I'm gwine to Alabamy, *Oh* . . .
> For to see my manny, *Ah* . . .
> She went from Ole Virginny, *Oh* . . .
> And I'm her pickaninny, *Ah* . . .
> She lives on the Tombigbee, *Oh* . . .
> I wish I had her wid me, *Ah* . . .[17]

Each individual developed his or her own unique cry, to which the rest would respond appropriately, although there were of course some particularly talented "leaders." Such songs helped to make the long hours of work more bearable to the slaves, and were an aid to them in tasks requiring them to work in rhythm together. Masters and overseers welcomed any device that contributed to the slaves' work efficiency, and did not, apparently, notice that the songs were often satirical and replete with *double-entendre*.

Work songs, mood songs, taunt songs, chants—each form evolved to express a different feeling, but within each form resided a plethora of variations of feeling. Even simple Western songs taught to the slaves were embellished with cries and moans in a manner quite inexplicable to their white owners. Their songs were always marked by a syncopated vocal or rhythmic line. First generation slaves had difficulty mastering the Western scale, for their own musical heritage, particularly the "blue notes" or areas in the scale where tones are smeared together, interfered. Succeeding generations learned the Western scale but retained through the tradition of plantation songs the African musical forms.[18] Thus, it was possible for Jiles Joplin, when he was a slave, to play one night at his owner's home the waltzes, schottisches and quadrilles familiar to the white guests and the next night to accompany his fellow slaves in renditions of plantation songs.

In Texarkana, Scott Joplin heard the plantation songs and felt the plantation rhythms freshly imported from the river bottom country to the east; and he heard those, altered by time and Northern influence, that his mother played on her banjo and sang. At a very early age he was able to pick out these songs on his mother's banjo, on which he was proficient by the age of seven.

A further, and very important, influence on young Scott Joplin was the black church, an institution still in its infancy in the former slave states were separate black worship had been outlawed prior to the Civil War. Whites feared the slaves would use their churches as meeting places and centers of unrest, and slaves had been traditionally provided certain sections in the white churches, or separate services. One of the earliest manifestations of the slaves' recognition of their new status as freedmen had been their withdrawal from white churches and the establishment of their own. The general reaction among whites was consternation and contempt, for black religion was considered "woefully mixed with ignorance and superstition."[19]

There was considerable superstition in the black subculture, a combination of carry-overs from the African past, adaptations of white, European myths, and misconceptions of the prevailing white religions. Denied full access to organized religion and faced with an otherwise inexplicably harsh existence, the slaves had developed a rich folklore of magical and mystical elements, of superstition and conjuration. That Scott Joplin was exposed to superstition as a child is evident in his opera *Treemonisha*, a major theme of which is the conquering of superstition by education. To which particular superstitions he was exposed is not known, but it is likely that in the black community of Texarkana at that time illness was attributed to being "crossed" or "hoodooed" by an enemy, graveyard dust was considered an exceptionally powerful substance, and one's front steps were important for a variety of reasons: enemies tended to bury charms under them, so they had to be examined frequently; scrubbing them with special solutions brought good luck; washing them with urine protected the household. Borrowing or lending salt and pepper would break a friendship; sneezing in the morning foretold bad luck; a sore tongue meant a lie had been told. Few events or actions did not carry a plethora of hidden meanings.[20] Having been born free and in a northern state, Florence Joplin probably did not share many of these superstitions and instilled in her children her feeling that they helped to keep black people in poverty and ignorance.

The boundaries between black religion and black superstition in those days were fuzzy. Prayers were an integral part of some hoodoos, and mystical chants were often heard in religious ceremonies. Little wonder that whites looked down on black religion. There were few trained and educated black ministers, and black religion in this period was not only riddled with superstition but also charged with emotionalism.

The only black church in Texarkana was on the Texas side, at Fourth and Elm Streets. Mt. Zion Baptist Church had been established in 1875, and it served the black communities in both towns.[21] Like most black churches of the period it was a frame construction with twin towers on the front, contained about thirty by sixty feet of floor space, and was financed primarily by whites interested in the moral character of the freedmen.[22] In this church, Scott learned something about religion and a lot more about sound. He sat in the room when it was unpeopled and silent, and when it served as a social gathering place, members of the congregation greeting each other and exchanging pleasantries. He saw the same room come alive with religion, rocking with shouts, singing, the clapping of hands. He learned that a song with the most mournful theme could be accompanied and its sadness intensified by a persistent, staccato clapping. And in church, as in the outside black community, once he had apprehended the larger significance of race, he learned and understood the ways black people had caused the white Christian religion to work for them during slavery, to use their spirituals to convey literal messages, such as this one sung when an escaped slave was being pursued by bloodhounds:

> Wade in the water, wade in the water
> Children, God gonna trouble the water.[23]

He learned, too, that in church as well as outside it, wherever possible his people turned a song into a dance, for the rhythm of tapping feet and moving bodies was considered essential to the expression of religious feeling. One of the most popular of these forms was the ring shout, described by an observer in 1867. ". . . all stand up in the middle of the floor, and when the 'sperichil' is struck up, begin first walking and by-and-by shuffling round, one after the other, in a ring. The foot is hardly taken from the floor, and the progression is mainly due to a jerking, hitching motion which agitates the entire shouter, and soon brings out streams of perspiration. Sometimes he dances silently, sometimes as he shuffles he sings the chorus of the spiritual, and sometimes the song itself is also sung by the dancers. But more frequently a band, composed of some of the best singers and of tired shouters, stand at the side of the room to 'base' the others, singing the body of the song and clapping their hands together or on their knees. Song and dance alike are extremely energetic . . ."[24] Like the other children, Scott was encouraged to participate and could shout at any time. The adults, more mindful of the religious meaning of the shout, refrained unless sincerely overcome by religious fervor.[25]

The ring shouts and spirituals, the work songs and blues songs, his mother's banjo playing, his father's fiddling—the varied musical stimulation to which Scott Joplin was exposed as a small child is enviable. Had he been purposely taught the Western European musical forms and the rhythms and blue notes so strongly rooted in the African tradition, he would have been incapable of absorbing it all. But these forms were part of his milieu; he learned them hardly aware that he was learning. They were everywhere around him, just as they had been for the generations of Southern black children who had gone before. But Scott showed a particular musical propensity,

one that distinguished him even from his musically talented brothers and sisters. In the small black community
of Texarkana, Scott's talent was noticed and spoken of
and attracted the attention of area music teachers, who
offered to instruct him.

One was Mag Washington, a black woman who lived
on Laurel Street and who later taught music at the first
black schools in the town. Another was J. C. Johnson, a
small man variously remembered as a mulatto, a Mexican,
"Indian looking" and partly of German descent, who engaged in an equally wide range of enterprises. He was a
barber (there were no white barbers in Texarkana at the
time and barbering was considered a Negro trade), a real
estate trader who eventually owned more real estate than
any other black in Texarkana, a musician, and a music
teacher. His home on Wood Street was only three or four
blocks away from the Joplin residence, and there, in his
neat small house, he would give music lessons on the
piano, violin, and horn,[26] the strains wafting over his fan-
shaped wooden gate and out into the neighborhood. Because he was a musician and music teacher he enjoyed
the title Professor and was addressed in this manner by
both blacks and whites.[27] Johnson played in the classical
style. "He was a kind of church man," recalls elderly Texarkana resident George Mosley. "He didn't play much
ragtime (later), and I don't think he played at dances. A
lot of people had guitars or fiddles, but his music was not
like most."[28] From these early music teachers, Scott Joplin
learned to read music and gained a better knowledge of
Western European musical forms, and because he was talented they taught him for little or no fee.

When he was not practicing his music, or being tutored
in academic subjects in the neighborhood, Scott did what

the other boys in the neighborhood did. He frequently ran errands, getting lunch for a laborer or water on a hot afternoon. He helped feed the chickens and pigs that most people kept in their yards, and when a flock of wild turkeys was driven through the town, he was often sent to purchase hens for people in the neighborhood. He played stickball in the street and dug in the ubiquitous sand and helped take care of his younger brothers and sisters. In the late spring of 1880, an epidemic of measles spread through the black section, infecting most of the young children. While ten-year-old Osie had primary responsibility for caring for the younger children, Will, four, and Myrtle, who had been born in March,[29] she, too, had contracted measles,[30] and at such times Scott and Robert took on the responsibility. Perhaps the crisis was welcome in some ways, for it helped take their minds off their parents and their problems. Jiles and Florence were not getting along. It is said that they argued over Scott. Jiles felt that Florence overencouraged their son's interest in music. Music was a fine pastime but certainly not a suitable vocation. Few black men he knew could make a respectable living at it. Scott's nephew, Fred Joplin, recalls that this attitude prevailed when he was young and dreamed of being like his uncle. "We don't want no piano player," his family said.[31] But it is unlikely that the disagreement over Scott was the cause of their separation, as legend would have it. Whatever the reasons, Jiles left Florence and the children in the latter half of 1880 or the early part of 1881, when Scott was twelve or thirteen years old.[32] He moved to a boardinghouse on Laurel Street on the Arkansas side and entered into another marriage-like relationship with a woman named Laura. But he maintained close contact with the family.

By the time Jiles left his family, Texarkana had progressed substantially. Jay Gould passed through the town in March of 1880. "Texarkana will grow," he informed Mayor Beidlee. The town had an opera house and brick buildings, a newspaper, and many stump-free streets. A month after Gould's visit, it had its first Bath Rooms, installed in the rear of the white-managed City Barber Shop. Hot Baths were 25¢, Cold 20¢, Salt 25¢, Sulphur 50¢. Blacks enjoyed some freedoms. In the year 1881–82, half the men who served on juries were black. But neither material nor social progress affected Florence Joplin to any great extent. Left with the responsibility of five children aged twelve down to infancy (Monroe had a job as a cook and had moved out before Jiles left), she concentrated on providing for them. While she had earned money previously by taking in washing and ironing,[33] it was not enough to support her family.

Probably to find less expensive living quarters, she moved her family over to the larger black section on the Arkansas side of Texarkana, to the area called Near-Town and to a house at 618 Hazel Street on the corner of Sixth.[34] The area was one of sand flats, the sand so deep that you bogged down in it when you walked; and as it was at the foot of a hill extending downward from the east, it flooded every time there were heavy rains. In the late spring it was a veritable mud flat.[35] The house at 618 Hazel was on the edge of the black section, in a neighborhood that was quite racially integrated. While blacks lived on the even-numbered side of the street, mostly whites lived on the odd-numbered side.[36]

At about the same time Florence and her young children moved, the infant and still informally organized Canaan Baptist Church also moved from Mrs. Samuels' parlor on

Eighth Street to the recently evacuated Dyckman Hide house on Ash and East Ninth Street. It was not a church building per se, but it was large and roomy and far better suited to the needs of the congregation than Mrs. Samuels' parlor. The members made simple board benches and fashioned a makeshift pulpit and looked forward to the time when, new members having been attracted by the existence of a separate building in which to worship, Canaan would be officially recognized and organized by Mt. Zion.[37] Florence Joplin became caretaker of the church.[38]

Florence also worked as a domestic for white families in the area, among them the Cooks on Hazel Street. The Cooks owned a piano, and Florence realized here was an opportunity for Scott to practice on the instrument. She requested and received Mrs. Cook's consent to take Scott along when she went there to clean.[39] While his mother dusted and mopped around him, young Scott sat on the high bench of the Cooks' upright in the parlor and practiced the scales his teachers had taught him. As he grew bolder, he began to try his hand at playing the sheet music the Cooks had—sentimental ballads by Stephen Foster, perhaps, minstrel tunes, folios of European piano music, and undoubtedly a march by John Philip Sousa, whose music was becoming immensely popular all over the country. And as he grew bolder still, perhaps he experimented with tunes of his own. He was blessed with two characteristics important to a composer/musician. He had perfect pitch. If a chord were struck on a piano in the next room, Scott could walk into the room and duplicate the chord exactly.[40] He also had the ability to remember tunes and fragments of tunes that he had heard years before. Already he was taking those remembered tunes and incorporating them, with elements of his own, into original compositions.

Scott was probably a teen-ager before he was able to go to an actual school building for black students. Although a relatively good public school system had been established in Texarkana for white students, a school for black children came only later.[41] Located in a frame building on Seventh Street and the Kansas City Southern tracks on the Texas side about ten blocks from Scott's home, the school was called Central High School, although the "high" part was purely honorary. There would be no upper grades for some years. Later, a small brick building was erected to house the school. Consisting of one aboveground story and a basement, it was typical of the accommodations for black students at the time. Below street level, the building's grounds and basement were frequently flooded after heavy rains, necessitating rescue operations by parents. Fill was then added to bring the school grounds up to street level and the drainage canal was levied to check flooding. Another, more spacious building was erected. Students were placed in grades according to their age rather than their educational level, a practice that continued until a centralized state public school system was firmly established,[42] and thus if Scott attended Central High he was probably placed in seventh or eighth grade. There were no extracurricular activities,[43] but in this era so soon after Emancipation parents were eager for proof that their children were indeed securing the magic key called education, and there were numerous assemblies and programs to assure them. If Scott Joplin attended the school, it is likely that he was a sort of musician-in-residence and served as musical accompanist at assemblies, whether indoor activities or outdoor programs such as the annual plaiting of the May-pole.[44] Whether or not Joplin attended the later Orr School will be discussed shortly.

Despite her poor economic circumstances and difficulty in supporting her family, Florence Joplin purchased a piano, primarily for Scott's use.[45] While this was an extravagance for a poor family, it was not an uncommon one. Music was the chief entertainment in that era, and even some of the poorest homes boasted a piano, usually secondhand. Probably the one Florence purchased was a used model and an old square-type piano in which the strings were parallel to the keys as in the clavichord. Sheet music could be purchased at the Beasley Music Store for five cents and ten cents, and Scott began spending most of the money he earned doing errands and odd jobs in the neighborhood to buy the popular sheet music of the day. Florence Joplin considered her purchase a worthwhile investment, for she had little doubt that her second son was destined for a musical career. Already he was well known in the Texarkana area, and in this era when black people grasped with clawing fingers at whatever renown they might enjoy, talent like his was to be encouraged.

There were many opportunities for a young black musician to perform in an East Texas town in those days. Most blacks were poor and their lives monotonous, a situation that became more severe with increasing political repression. Correspondingly, the freedmen sought greater solidarity among themselves and more social diversions. The black church became increasingly the center of black social as well as religious life. In the cities, blacks organized fire companies, benevolent societies, fraternal societies (The Grand United Order of Odd Fellows for Negroes was organized in Texas before 1879). Several lodge halls were located in Texarkana's sand flat. Lodge meetings would be held until about 10 P.M., whereupon the hall would be turned over to the young people for dancing. The music was similar to that played at dances for whites —polkas, schottisches, waltzes, and two-steps.[46] Baseball teams, literary, dramatic, and debating societies—every town of any size had its diversions. On weekends blacks from outlying areas arrived to purchase supplies and enjoy the company of other blacks. The towns were sites of numerous festivities throughout the year. The most important were Emancipation Day and Fourth of July, but there were also celebrations at the end of the harvest season and the close of the school year, railroad excursions, and school and church picnics.

Scott Joplin performed at church socials and school functions, later for black clubs. "He was smart," Zenobia Campbell, now deceased, recalled, "especially in music . . . He did not have to play anybody else's music. He made up his own, and it was beautiful; he just got his music out of the air."[47]

Still later, he played at area dance halls, including that of Webster Crow, a dance teacher, and one on Law Street. All the while, he was listening to and absorbing into his own idiom the marches, the popularizations of the musical forms of the black church, the minstrel songs and semblances of the blues that were sung and played by other area entertainers. He also probably heard the currently popular tunes played in syncopated style, most notably those of composer Louis Moreau Gottschalk, whose composition *The Banjo* contained clever banjo imitations and was very popular at the time. Alexander Ford felt sure he had heard Scott play the music found in "Maple

Leaf Rag" in Texarkana before he began playing in the larger cities. "Scott worked on his music all the time. He was a musical genius. He didn't need a piece of music to go by. He played his own music without anything."[48]

Scott was a small young man of medium-dark complexion who looked remarkably like his father but who had far more ambition than the older man. He yearned to make a living in music and to escape the conditions under which blacks in East Texas lived. Black boys his age had few opportunities in the Texarkana area. The only employment open to them was railroad work, jobs in the lumber camps and sawmills, or domestic and personal services. Scott's older brother, Monroe, had gotten a job with a railroad. "He would ride as far as Marshall, and stay there two or three days; then he would come in and take the very next train out to Marshall," according to Alexander Ford. As a porter, he could pass through any area of the train, but had he attempted to ride as a passenger he would have been confined to the "Colored" section. In the lumber camps and sawmills, blacks were assigned the most menial and distasteful jobs, and had no hope for promotion or increased responsibility. Scott had no liking for manual labor. He was also a proud young man who did not wish to spend his life serving whites. He admired his music teacher, J. C. Johnson, and emulated him in some ways—in his quiet pride, in his liking for soft and gentle tunes, in his awareness of the importance of education. But J. C. Johnson was an excellent businessman. His real estate investments had already made him one of the wealthiest blacks in Texarkana. Scott, on the other hand, had little head for business and less interest in it. Besides, he did not wish to spend the rest of his life in Texarkana. The excitement he must have felt as a small boy about the coming of the railroad and the endless possibilities for travel that it represented had remained with him and matured into a desire to see what was at the other end of the line. And thus, while other boys his age played and partied, aware that there was no future and that the present was all, Scott Joplin kept to himself and practiced his music. "Scott was earnest," Zenobia Campbell remembered. "When a bunch of boys got together on a spree one night and asked Scott to go with them, he said, 'No sir, I won't have anything to do with such foolishness. I'm going to make a man out of myself.'"[49]

For this reason, among others, it is probable that Scott attended school longer than most boys his age. The theme of *Treemonisha* and Joplin legend both indicate that his mother and later Joplin himself believed deeply in the importance of education. Also, there is evidence that Joplin was fairly well educated. He later enrolled in the music school in Sedalia, read such books as Lewis Carroll's *Alice's Adventures in Wonderland*, wrote well enough to have a brief statement published in a New York newspaper. At least one Joplin family friend claimed to remember Joplin's attending Orr School, located on the corner of Ninth and Laurel on the Arkansas side of town. It was organized in 1886 and established in 1887, when Scott was eighteen or nineteen years old. But Zenobia Campbell recalled, "It was in the old two-story building. The little kids like me went downstairs, but the big high school kids went upstairs. Scott was in high school upstairs when I was little and went downstairs."[50] Although Scott would have been one of the oldest in the school, there would have been little stigma involved. He was something of a celebrity within the black community, a serious and intense young man about whom older blacks nodded and assured each other that he would go far.

Scott was also known in the white community and in the surrounding towns. When he was about sixteen, he had formed a vocal group, the Texas Medley Quartette, with his brother Will and two neighborhood boys, Wesley Kirby and Tom Clark. After their first engagement in Clarksville, Texas, about eighty miles west of Texarkana, they secured engagements elsewhere and, though they retained their original name, took on a fifth member, Robert Joplin. The group played in and around the area for some four years, and the money they earned was welcome in the Joplin household.[51] But Scott Joplin had bigger plans, and around 1898, when he was twenty, he left Texarkana to seek his musical fortune.[52]

CHAPTER III

Itinerant Pianist

At that time a throng of itinerant pianists crisscrossed the South and the Midwest by train and river steamer, by wagon and on foot, performing wherever they could and for whatever they could get. They were in great demand in those days, when sources of musical entertainment were few and the arrival of a traveling performer or minstrel show was a notable event in a small town. Up and down the Mississippi River they traveled, and over into Kansas and Missouri, Oklahoma and Nebraska and Texas, in a time when these areas were in a constant state of flux. Hundreds of people were traveling westward in railroad cars, covered wagons, buggies, buckboards, on horseback and muleback. A few even rode big, high-wheeled bicycles. There was a fever in the country—a fever for cheap farmland and the independence that land ownership could offer to these mostly poor travelers. The Government was opening up former Indian territory for settlement, and people from older states were heading westward searching for new opportunity.[1]

Enterprising businessmen established trading posts and general stores to serve the needs of these travelers. Traveling salesmen and hucksters schemed to relieve them of their small savings. Itinerant entertainers were everywhere. They rode the paddle-wheelers up and down the rivers and stopped at riverbank taverns. They barnstormed with small minstrel and variety shows and accompanied medicine men, attracting a crowd with their music before the "Doctor" or "Professor" appeared to convince his audience how sorely they needed his homemade elixir. They accompanied tent shows to the small towns and frequented the saloons and honky-tonks in the large population centers, and over the years they formed a musical subculture.

They represented a variety of geographical and musical backgrounds. Some had been trained in European musical forms; some had not. Some could read music; others could not. They were from the South, the West, the Midwest, and the North, and as they affected the area around the Mississippi Valley, so that area affected them. They learned the folk songs and dances of the people for whom they played, added to them their own folk songs and dances, their hymns, and included, too, the marches, dances, and tunes from popular sheet music to produce an amalgamation of assorted forms and themes which over the years had taken on a rather distinct form, an extended melodic line of syncopations in conjunction with a regularly metered bass.

Neither they nor their music was socially acceptable. They existed on the fringes—of towns, of society—and yet it was this very semioutcast status that gave them a sense of belonging to each other. They shared a love of music, of travel, of new experiences—a commonality that over-

shadowed whatever differences separated them. They
ranged from little more than adolescents to old-timers in
their sixties and seventies. They were mostly black, but
by the late 1880s there were also a considerable number
of whites.

The two groups of itinerants, the whites and blacks,
existed sometimes separately, sometimes together, within
the same milieu. Rather like a double helix, they separated, then came together, then separated again according to the social and geographical environment through
which they happened to be traveling. Often their paths
paralleled each other, as did the social lives of their respective audiences. Both lower-class blacks and lower-
class whites engaged in similar yet separate socializing.
Both had their fairs and their excursions, their dances and
lodge outings. In the towns, Saturday was the day when
people from the countryside would come to do their shop-
ping or selling and then linger on into the evening to attend a dance or patronize a local drinking or gambling establishment in the white or black section of town
according to their own racial heritage. The traveling musicians, appearing singly or in groups of two or three,
were essential to all these activities, whether among the
poorer classes of blacks or the poorer classes of whites.
The better classes of both races, the straitlaced, conser-
vative, churchgoing pillars of their respective communities, had their own bands and string orchestras, and had
little use for the musical drifters. Only Negro groups like
the Fisk (University) Jubilee Singers, who began touring
in 1871 and were highly successful, gained entree to the
better classes of black and white society.

In the larger towns the white and black itinerants came
together. The well-established red-light districts in these

towns sported a minimum of segregation. White or black, a talented musician was a talented musician, a charming madam was a charming madam, and a man with money to spend was a welcome sight. Blacks and whites in these districts were all outcasts of one sort or another, and racism seemed rather beside the point.

Life was never monotonous for the traveling musician. Arriving in a small town, he was likely to set up on a side-walk corner and play for coins tossed at his feet, until he was hired to play for a picnic or a railroad or steamboat excursion. Hearing of a fair or a race in some other town, he would set out for it, walking or riding the train or steamboat depending on his financial circumstances at the moment. On the way, he might meet up with a medicine show whose owner was looking for a musical pitch-man, and find himself traveling in a direction quite different from the one on which he had set out that morning. Nearing one of the larger towns, he might leave the show to spend a few weeks in an established red-light district. He lived from day to day and from hand to mouth. At times, he would play almost continuously for three days or more and have money for a woman, for a keg of beer and a bag full of food. At other times, he would be so broke he would have to play for his supper or sleep in a corncrib. If he was near a larger town or city, he would try to sell a quick song or tune to a local music publisher. It might not be entirely his composition, but then the music of the itinerant musician in those days was an amalgam of influences and styles, of melodies heard in the fields and songs picked up on the levees and phrases picked out on barroom pianos. Every itinerant in those days was a composer in a sense, and the traveling musicians, white and black, sharing their ideas with each other, learning from one another, also shared the musical idiom that had already become known as ragtime, for music played in "ragged time."[2]

The term *ragged time* is a colloquialism for syncopation, the placing of emphasis in the melodic line where it would not be expected to fall in a "straight" rendering of a piece, and it was the syncopation of the music that had the greatest impact on the unschooled white listener in the late 1880s. Even though syncopation is not the defining element of ragtime, it differed so radically from European rhythms and the popular arrangements of folk tunes that it must have been positively shocking. Yet to us nearly a century later, a period of decades that has seen the development of jazz and rock music, the syncopation of ragtime seems quite tame. Indeed, even then it was far tamer than that of the forms out of which it grew, most notably the staccato clapping that often accompanied songs sung in Negro churches and the foot-produced drum sounds of plantation dances.[3]

The term *ragtime* was not then nor is it today a particularly appropriate label, being far too simplistic in definition. But there is no one-word definition that adequately defines the form. Ragtime is essentially a collection and integration of little melodies, played in a manner similar to the way in which black plantation and church songs were sung and black plantation dances were performed, all of which forms included syncopation but were not determined by it. There is also no smooth developmental line on which one can pinpoint the emergence of ragtime —no single predecessor or successor in the evolution of distinctly American music. It represents an amalgamation of forms and trends. The one identifiable pattern it follows is that it conforms to the custom in American music of interracial influence. Whites adapt black forms which are in turn adapted and parodied by blacks, which are once again adapted and parodied by whites, not always with the most sympathetic intentions.

Minstrelsy represents an excellent example of this process, and ragtime owes much to the minstrel tradition. The roots of minstrelsy lie in the plantation slave quarters, which inevitably had a talented individual or band that could sing and dance to the accompaniment of the banjo, the tambourine, and the "bones" (ribs of a sheep or other small animal) and tell jokes. These individuals and bands frequently entertained for their masters and fellow slaves, and some became semiprofessional, although their travel was circumscribed during the slavery period. At the same time, white entertainers were traveling wider and whiter circuits, but inevitably they came into contact with the Negro groups. Negro mannerisms and customs being inherently funny to whites, the white entertainers began to adapt them for comic appeal. As early as 1810, blackface impersonations were being presented by what can best be described as circus clown-type performers, although the modern circus had not as yet been organized. By the next decade, solo blackface acts with the traditional slave instruments had become popular. The use of these percussive instruments, the banjo, tambourine, and bones, helped to establish the rhythmic foundation of later minstrel shows.[4]

Minstrelsy in the form with which we are most familiar began around 1828–29 when, according to legend, an actor named Thomas Rice included in his act the song and dance of an old black man who worked in the stable next to the Louisville theater where Rice was appearing.

Edmon S. Connor, who claimed to have been an eyewitness to this birth of minstrelsy, recalled:

As was then usual with slaves, they called themselves after their owner, so that old Daddy had assumed the name of Jim Crow. He was very much deformed, the right shoulder being drawn up high, the left leg stiff and crooked at the knee, giving him a painful, but at the same time laughable limp. He used to croon a queer old tune with words of his own, and at the end of each verse would give a little jump, and when he came down he set his "heel a-rockin'." He called it "jumping Jim Crow." The words of the refrain were:

> "Wheel about, turn about,
>   Do jis so,
> An' ebry time I wheel about,
>   I jump Jim Crow!"[5]

Intrigued and amused, Rice adapted the character of Jim Crow for his act, using not only the old man's song and his funny little dance but also his name. Thomas Rice became known professionally as Daddy 'Jim Crow' Rice. "Jump Jim Crow" was an immediate hit, in the United States as well as in Europe, and Rice's act spawned a host of imitations,[6] almost exclusively white actors in blackface. Parodies of Negro songs became popular sellers in sheet music. Stephen Foster was perhaps the most successful composer in this genre. By the middle of the century troupes of white entertainers were traveling the circuits presenting blackface performances that included music, dancing, and jokes, the full minstrel show that was the precursor of vaudeville.

Minstrelsy enjoyed its Golden Age from about 1850 to

1875. During that time, though the minstrels' material consisted of adaptations and parodies of Negro music and mannerisms, they adapted it creatively and with some sympathy. There was in these imitations a certain sense of poignancy and romanticism about the slave and his life (although this hardly benefited the slave, since it glorified the slave regime) and a freshness that would be lost in the post-Civil War period.

By about 1875 ministrelsy had lost its creative spark. Since Emancipation, black entertainers had enjoyed more freedom of movement and been allowed onto the minstrel circuits, but minstrelsy had become so formularized by that time that even the black minstrels performed in blackface. The wit, imagination, and brightness of early minstrelsy had degenerated into a standard routine of not particularly funny jokes, wooden dancing, and undistinguished songs, and while the emphasis on so-called Negro characteristics, mannerisms, and speech idioms was stronger than ever, there were no longer clever adaptations but unimaginative parodies. Perhaps partly in an effort to enliven the form, and partly in response to the social upheaval caused by Emancipation and the Reconstruction period, minstrelsy became harsher in its Negro characterizations, and it was this period that fixed in the white American mind the unfortunate stereotype of the Negro as happy-go-lucky, dancing, shuffling, irresponsible, etcetera.[7]

While the minstrel shows were variety presentations and not primarily associated with musical performance, they affected the itinerant musicians. Lay audiences, accustomed to the style of minstrelsy, often demanded it of the musicians who played for them, a confining and frustrating position for the musicians exposed to a wealth of musical styles and creative possibilities. And for the black itinerant musician the minstrel-engendered black stereotypes were a difficult cross to bear. For a serious young man like Scott Joplin, they must have provided some impetus to present Negro musical idioms with the dignity and understanding they deserved. By the mid-1890s blacks would infuse minstrelsy with a new creativity. In the middle and late 1880s itinerant black musicians had already begun this rescue process, by adapting elements of rhythm and swing in minstrelsy to the ragtime form.

Ragtime can also be related to Negro songs and Negro-influenced songs—not to their words or tunes but to their form. Traditional slave songs were fluid in form, or open-ended, for their purpose was to communicate the feelings of the moment. The call-mass response form of work songs and many spirituals depended greatly on the effectiveness of the leader, the inflection of whose call would produce a corresponding inflection in each chorus.[8] Calls and choruses related in subject matter to one theme, but potential variations were endless, and the more effective the leader the more varied but related the verses.

> Jordan River, I'm bound to go,
>   Bound to go, bound to go,—
> Jordan River, I'm bound to go,
>   And bid 'em fare ye well.
>
> My Brudder Robert, I'm bound to go,
>   Bound to go, etc.
>
> My Sister Lucy, I'm bound to go,
>   Bound to go, etc.[9]

White minstrels had adapted the Negro song form but introduced theme combinations that blacks would never have used. The following is obviously a gross parody of a black spiritual:

> Monkey dressed in soldier clothes
> All cross over Jordan
> Went in de woods to drill some crows
> O Jerusalem—[10]

Yet the call-mass response form was maintained, introduced to, and accepted by the general audience, and later appeared in ragtime. In rag the composer/performer essentially plays the part of both leader and chorus, his effectiveness dependent upon his skill at inflecting the various choruses. In plantation songs, each chorus is unique in the manner in which it introduces and develops the theme and relates to the other choruses.[11] Rag, too, is open-ended and was particularly so in this early period of ragtime, before the music was actually written down. Effectiveness of communication was more important than structural perfection.

Musicologist Addison W. Reed has suggested a further relationship between black vocal forms and ragtime. "One may notice particularly the melodic rise at the end of a spiritual which automatically lets one know that we have or are approaching the end, the same may be said for the 'ride-out' (grandiose ending) of a rag. And the changing character of a holler or work song may be compared to the rhetoric of each chorus of a classic rag . . . It may be argued that the very nature of the introductions, closing sections, bridges and codettas (of a rag) relate to the vocal forms of the Negro . . . Just as the introduction to a rag denotes the mood, the same can be said for the leader of a spiritual. As the closing sections and codettas add an additional phrase which compliments the preceding chorus, so did the leader in his emphasis of what the congregation had previously sung. The same may be said of bridges since they provide a link between two related passages, as did the leader and so was the function of the call in relation to the response."[12]

Work songs and hollers, spirituals and blues, the percussive rhythms of the banjo and bones—all contributed in some way to the development of ragtime. But the most important basis of ragtime is dance music—particularly black dance music. In some ways, it was the character of the life of the itinerant pianist that led to the development of ragtime. The wine rooms and saloons, the cafes and bawdyhouses where they played were often transient, fly-by-night affairs, known neither for their permanence nor their opulence. Entertainment "budgets" in these places were small, the chief investment being a single piano. Musicians who played other instruments of course furnished their own, but rarely was anything more than a small combo provided. The chief entertainment was the lone pianist, who worked not for a guaranteed salary but for whatever tips he could get. In return, he was called upon to provide a variety of musical entertainment—background music, music to sing by, and especially dance music. Over in respectable society, a dance band would be available. In the red-light districts, the piano was all, and the most popular and successful musicians were those whose music made their listeners *want* to dance, *want* to tap their feet and move their bodies to its rhythms.

Naturally, this music also had to conform to the types

of dances that the audience wanted to do and that were in vogue. The popularity of marches, most notably those by John Philip Sousa, had spawned the two-step. In fact, that dance became identified with a Sousa march, the *Washington Post March*, so thoroughly that it was often called *The Washington Post*.[13]

Blacks, as was their custom and their irresistible impulse, had subsequently adapted and amended the two-step and created the "cakewalk." Originating in the South around 1880, its primary characteristic was promenading in an exaggeratedly dignified manner. Contests were held among blacks for which the prize was usually a cake, giving rise to the expression "That takes the cake." By the mid-90s, whites had in turn adopted the cakewalk and white composers would make a fortune selling cakewalk sheet music. More fluid and imaginative than the established two-step, the cakewalk was nevertheless a regularized form, one that allowed for more improvisational possibilities than its precursors but that would be considered highly formalized compared to later dance styles such as the Charleston, Black Bottom and Lindy Hop.

Black folk dances were also popular in evolved form. Originating in the United States in plantation slave quarters (and undoubtedly containing elements of African tribal dances, although this is difficult to document), these dances were first brought to the attention of the larger white public via the white minstrel shows and were then reprocessed through the black imagination to be accepted first by the low-class segments of white society and eventually by all classes. Ragtime incorporated all these dance traditions, and dancing was its primary impulse. A piano rag was like a keyboard dance suite in-

74

tended to inspire and accompany expressive physical motion.[14]

Just when and by whom the first piano rag phrase was played will never be known, for this was a time when music went unrecorded except in the ears and minds of its listeners. It is likely that certain rag elements were present in the playing of itinerant pianists many years before the ragtime style seemed to coalesce and become a recognizable form in the 1890s. In 1892, Tony Jackson, a New Orleans Negro pianist, composed a tune called "Michigan Waters" that contained some elements that could be classified as ragtime, and the next year, 1893, the word "ragtime" appeared for the first time on a sheet music cover—Fred Stone, a Negro musician in Detroit, published "Ma Ragtime Baby." It will be remembered also that an old-timer in Texarkana believed that he had heard parts of "Maple Leaf Rag" even before Joplin left the town to strike out on his own.

Scott Joplin joined the ranks of the itinerant musicians who moved across the South and West developing the music that would become ragtime. It is not known where he went or how long he roamed. It is likely that he caught the excitement of the frontier West, the rush for land, the influx of people from more established sections of the country. He probably encountered the Indians who traveled some forty thousand strong to Arkansas City from Indian Territory every three months to receive their government allotments, paid to them through the First National Bank of Arkansas City. By day they traveled, most of them walking, wrapped in blankets; at night they set up their camps along the riverbanks.[15] In another era, they might have presented quite a spectacle, but in those days they were simply a part of the phenomenon that was the frontier West.

Eventually, Joplin made his way to Missouri, where he settled for a time in St. Louis, probably about 1890. A large, sprawling city known as the "Gateway to the West," in its variety and bustle St. Louis resembled a seaport, although it was far from the sea. The major population center of the Midwest, it fronted on the Mississippi and thus had naturally become one of the chief commercial centers for the river traffic from and to the South. Railroads had joined the river byways, and by the time of Joplin's arrival the city had become the Midwestern center for rail as well as riverboat travel.

By 1900, blacks in St. Louis would number 35,516, or 6.17 per cent of the population. They were concentrated within two of the city's ten wards, but within these wards there was considerable residential and social variety. The higher class boasted its own social and literary clubs and church-sponsored entertainment, its own brilliantly uniformed bands, and its own lodges and fraternal organizations. Still, members of this class were rarely seen at a downtown theater or even at one of the summer gardens, resorts which were popular among all classes of white society. The mass of St. Louis blacks had their railroad and steamboat excursions, barbecues, cakewalks, picnics and church sociables, once again, entirely segregated affairs. And then there were the low-class blacks, among them the operators of saloons, who were probably financially better off than some of the upper-class blacks. By 1901, St. Louis blacks would own eleven saloons, representing a capital investment of $17,000, employing a total of forty-eight people. Wrote a white observer at the time: "The saloons are perhaps the most profitable enterprises engaged in. One has been established since 1879 and has $5,000 invested in it . . . The color line seems not to be drawn among their clientele, but the white customers are, of course, of the lowest class."[16]

About half of these black-owned and operated saloons were located in the city's sporting district, a section not far from the waterfront and near the Union Railroad Station, whose main thoroughfares were Chestnut and Market Streets. A rather large section, as befits a city that called itself the "Gateway to the West," it boasted numerous saloons, cafes, cheap boardinghouses and brothels, among the most colorful of which was Babe Connors' place. According to S. Brunson Campbell, the most beautiful and elegant black women were to be had there, and their pimps, or "Macks," were equally glamorous. Supported in style by their women, they dressed in silks and diamonds, sported jewelry made from twenty-dollar gold pieces, and spent most of their time showing off their finery and checking up on their women. Ragtime was the music played at Babe Connors' place, and Campbell recalled that Scott Joplin's compositions would be heard there before they were set down on paper.[17]

As in every red-light district, there were certain establishments in Chestnut Valley that the musicians frequented, although they might be performing elsewhere. One of the newest and most popular of these was the Silver Dollar Saloon at 425 South Twelfth Street, owned and operated by black "Honest John" Turpin, a pianist himself and a former laborer who had opened his saloon in 1890 with his three sons, Robert, Charles, and Thomas.[18] Here at almost any hour of the day or night St. Louis's piano players could be found, waiting for a messenger from some other establishment to come looking for a musician, playing for one another, and talking about music. Not long after arriving in St. Louis, Scott Joplin found the Silver Dollar, and for the next seven years he was to be a constant visitor to the saloon, which would serve as one of the most important "schools" he would ever attend.

There was constant competition among the musicians who frequented the Silver Dollar, and though they were as supportive as a family to young and talented new-comers, they were also the harshest of critics to those whose pretensions outweighed their skill or creativity. One had to earn the respect of the Silver Dollar crowd, and by all accounts Scott Joplin did so. He particularly impressed his fellow musicians with his improvisational and compositional abilities, skills he had shown even as a youngster in Texarkana. He also became close friends with John L. Turpin and his sons, who functioned at least officially as bartenders at the Silver Dollar.

They were large, burly young men. Some years before, Charles and Thomas had tried their hand at mining, and had spent some time at the Big Onion Mine in Search-light, Nevada,[19] and they often regaled their listeners with stories of their adventures. They contrasted sharply with the slightly built, quiet Scott Joplin, but they liked him immediately. It is said that he had a magnetic quality about him that attracted people to him. Tom Turpin shared Scott's interest in music and also aspired to a musical career. Within a short time, due to his being "talked up" by Turpin and other musicians, Joplin was able to play in other Chestnut Valley establishments as well as in surrounding towns and cities. The excellent transportation network around St. Louis made it possible for Joplin to make frequent brief trips to Hannibal, Carthage,

Columbia, and Sedalia and occasional longer journeys to Cincinnati and Louisville.

He always played in saloons and brothels, in the sporting districts of the cities he visited. As a young black man, he had few other forums for his music. One was the black church. Considering his quiet temperament and his desire for respectability, the church atmosphere might have suited him better, but it was impossible to make a living playing in churches. Besides, church music did not allow for Joplin's creativity. Such opportunities could only be found in the sporting districts. Another was one of the local black bands, but a musician had to be settled in a locality to play with such a band.

One could still dream, however, particularly when one's dream was shared by a friend. Tom Turpin, five years Joplin's junior, also wished for a more respectable career, one that would be creative and lucrative and not be confined to bawdyhouses and saloons. Like Scott, he was not merely a performer but a composer as well. In 1891 he listed himself in the St. Louis City Directory as a musician rather than as a bartender.

Scott did not list himself in the city directories at all, and it is likely that he was traveling a great deal at this time and perhaps staying with the Turpins at 1422 Market Street, or at 9 Targee Street, where they moved in 1892, or renting a room here and there in the Chestnut Valley District. He was not and did not consider himself sufficiently settled to advertise as Tom Turpin did. He traveled around, performing wherever he could. While doing so, he was picking up more work songs, more folk dances and idioms. As ragtime musician and historian Trebor Tichenor says, "Joplin was a musician who could store away things that he heard and bring them out later.

79

Classical European composers do this all the time, too,—take folk material and use it in their own style, in their own way."[20]

At the time, however, Joplin had no realistic aspirations to be a composer. Although he and Tom Turpin had often talked about composing in earnest and getting their compositions published, they, and particularly Scott, were highly aware of the odds against their ever doing so. At that time, few blacks had ever published. And then there was the problem of the type of music they played. It was associated with lowlife blacks, saloons, and bawdyhouses; it could hardly attract the mass market. It was not the sort of music that was generally written down. Scott could have written down his compositions and, according to legend, was urged to do so, but he did not. In a natural defensive reaction, he was not interested in doing anything he believed to be futile.

A turning point in Joplin's thinking and in his career seems to have occurred in 1893, when he journeyed to Chicago, site of the 1893 World's Columbian Exposition.[21] The very idea of a world's fair was still so new and exciting in the 1890s as to be difficult for later generations to understand. Anyone who could afford it, and many who couldn't, managed to visit the city that year, and accordingly anyone who could make money from that huge influx of people managed to get there, too. As was customary, the itinerant musicians were relegated to the fringes of the event, but as was also customary, they made the most of their opportunities on the fringe. A sporting district soon ringed the fairgrounds, providing, with Chicago's established tenderloin district from Eighteenth Street to the Illinois Central Railroad tracks, racy entertainment for the out-of-town visitors who could not

22		————	Delia	B	F	6	Daughter	1		
23		————	Fanny	B	F	2	Daughter	1		
24	261.343	Joplin	Giles	B	M	38			1	Common laborer	✓
25		————	Florence	B	F	39	Wife	1		Wash & Iron	✓
26		————	Munroe	B	M	19	Son	1		Works in Saw	—
27		————	Scott	B	M	12	Son	1		going to school	
28		————	Robt.	B	M	11	Son	1		do do	
29		————	Rosa	B	F	10	Daughter	1			
30		————	Willie	B	M	4	Son	1			
31		————	Johnny	B	M	7⁄12	Son	1			
32	262.344	McCalla	Gue Y.	W	M	74			1	Blacksmith	✓
33		————	Thos. P.	W	M	38	Son	1		R.R. Watchman	✓

The Joplin family entry in the census register of 1880 for Texarkana. *National Archives*

Scott Joplin, about 1900. This photograph appeared on the cover of "Swipesy— Cake Walk" (1900) and on the second cover of "Maple Leaf Rag." *New York Public Library*

***** Article of Agreement. *****

This agreement entered into this 10th day of August in the year of our
Lord 1899 by and between John Stark and son party of the first part and
Scott Joplin party of the second part both of the City of Sedalia and
County of Pettis and State of Missouri.

Witnesseth: That whereas Scott Joplin has composed a certain piece of
music entitled Maple Leaf Rag and has not funds sufficient to publish same
it is hereby agreed with above parties of the first part that John Stark
and son shall publish said piece of music and shall pay for all plates
and for copy right and printing and whatevr may be necessary to publish
said piece of music

It is further agreed by and between the parties hereto that John Stark and
son shall have the exclusive right to said piece of music to publish and s
sell and handle the same as they may seem fit and proper to their interest.

It is further agreed by and between the parties hereto that Scott
Joplins name shall appear in print on each and every piece of music as
composer and John Stark and son as publishers.

It is further agreed by and between the parties hereto that Scott Joplin
shall have free of charge ten copies of said piece of music as soon as
published.

It is further agreed by and between said parties that Scott Joplin the
composer of said music shall have and recieve a royalty of one cent per
copy on each copy of said piece of musi sold by said Stark and son.

It is further agreed by and between said parties that the said Scott
Joplin Shall be allowed to purchase and the said Stark and son agrees to
sell to the said Joplin all the copies of said music he may want at the
price of Five cents per copy be sold for less than Twent-five cents per
copy   said copies shall not
copy   said Joplin. It is further agreed that John Stark & Son
will not retail for less than Twenty five cents per copy.
Witness our hands and seals the day and year first above written.

John Stark & Son

Scott Joplin

Signed in presence of

R A Higdon

The original "Maple Leaf Rag" contract, August 10, 1899. Witness
R. A. Higdon claimed to have helped Joplin secure publication of
this composition. *The Maple Leaf Club*

Undoubtedly the most important man in Joplin's career, and one of the most important in his life, John Stark steadfastly supported classic ragtime even after the more commercialized Tin Pan Alley style gained prominence. *New York Public Library*

The Queen City Negro Band (later the Queen City Concert Band), about 1906. Italicized names indicate persons mentioned in the book. Unfortunately the J. Scott in the second row is not the composer. *Front row, l. to r.:* A. H. Hickman, R. O. Henderson, H. Martin, W. H. Carter, A. Wheeler, J. Stewart. *Second row:* W. Travis, J. Chisholm, J. Scott. *Third row: G. T. Ireland*, N. Diggs, E. Gravitt. *Last row:* C. W. Gravitt, *E. Cook. Fisk University Library Special Collections*

TO PLAY RAGTIME IN EUROPE

SCOTT JOPLIN.

Hitherto unpublished photograph of Joplin that appeared in the St. Louis *Post-Dispatch*, February 28, 1901, above an article about his proposed trip to Europe. *State Historical Society of Missouri*

Scott Joplin's piano, probably from his Missouri period. *Fisk University Library Special Collections*

have known to what a formidable array of talent they were privy. There, Scott met musicians whose experience was different from his own but whose ragged time music was similar in many respects. It broadened his perspective to learn that others, coming from different areas, could have adopted a similar musical form to express their experience. He was particularly impressed with two of Chicago's most prominent ragged time pianists, "Plunk" Henry Johnson and Johnny Seymour.

Joplin formed his first band in Chicago. It probably consisted of a cornet, clarinet, tuba, and a baritone horn. In arranging pieces for the band, he developed his instrumental notational ability.[22] He also met fellow pianist Otis Saunders, a native of Springfield, Missouri, and two years his junior, who was in Chicago for the fair. The two became close friends, and Saunders proved very important to Joplin, for he admired Joplin's piano compositions and convinced him to write them down.

No doubt Joplin had received such encouragement before, but his stay in Chicago probably was the first time when he began to believe that black music and music by blacks might have a chance at respectability. The *Creole Show*, an all-black revue which had opened in 1891, played a whole season at the World's Fair in 1893. Although its performers were veterans of the minstrel circuit, the show was anything but in their tired minstrelsy tradition. It broke tradition by dispensing with blackface and by emphasizing not only music but musical talent, bringing dancing and singing to the fore and de-emphasizing the banal jokes and skits. Another revitalized minstrel show played at the fair that year. W. C. Handy's "Mahara's Minstrels" incorporated strains of Memphis and Mississippi music never before heard in the music of a show. Scott Joplin recognized it, and he recognized, too, a new respectability accorded black music, a respectability still in its infancy, to be sure, but unmistakably present.

In 1894, Scott Joplin and Otis Saunders left Chicago and together made their leisurely way to St. Louis, stopping frequently to perform in saloons and cafes and bawdyhouses. They arrived back in St. Louis in late 1894 or early 1895 and found that the Turpins had established a new business. John now served as manager of Tom's new restaurant at the site of their former residence, 1422 Market Street, above which they now lived once again. Robert and Charles had gone their separate ways. Joplin confided to the Turpins that he had changed his mind. He had begun to write down some of his original compositions and intended to try to get them published. His experience at the World's Fair in Chicago had given him reason to be optimistic, and Otis Saunders had caused him to believe his work was good enough to sell, even if he was a Negro. Tom Turpin also decided to try to sell his compositions. It was a frightening but hopeful time for both young men. Joplin did not stay long in St. Louis. Whether it was wanderlust, or prodding from Saunders, or insecurity about his ability to write publishable compositions, he did not try to establish another band. Instead, he and Saunders continued on to Sedalia, Missouri, where in 1895 his brothers Robert and Will joined him.[23]

Scott had kept in touch with his family,[24] and his reports of the opportunities for traveling musical entertainers excited Robert and Will. Robert was about twenty-six and had worked for a time as a laborer in Texarkana, boarding at 830 Laurel Street with his father and Laura Joplin. Will was about nineteen and had been

working as a porter at the McCarthy Hotel in Texarkana.[25] Both had maintained their interest in music.
Will sang and played the violin and guitar, and Robert, in
addition to singing and playing several musical instruments, had also tried his hand at composing popular
songs. With Scott they revived the Texas Medley Quartette, which was not actually a quartet this time either
but an octet or double quartet. Scott served as leader,
conductor, and soloist. Robert sang baritone and Will
tenor. Other members were: John Williams, baritone;
Leonard Williams, tenor; Emmett Cook, tenor; Richard
Smith, bass; and Frank Bledsoe, bass. The group traveled
extensively under the auspices of Oscar Dame and the
Majestic Booking Agency. Toward the end of 1895 they
probably appeared in or around Syracuse, New York, for
Scott Joplin's first two songs were published in that city.[26]
Leiter Bros. published "A Picture of Her Face" and M. L.
Mantell issued "Please Say You Will," whose title page
bore the inscription "Song and Chorus by Scott Joplin of
the Texas Medley Quartette."[27]

Although both songs are well constructed and harmonized, they indicate Joplin's initial desire to "play it
safe" in attempting to get his work published. Neither
contains intimations of his later instrumental genius. Both
are typical sentimental ballads of the era, whose most
popular hit was "After the Ball," published in 1892 by
Charles K. Harris. Judging from the lyrics of the songs in
this genre, the Gay Nineties were misnamed. These were
the words Scott Joplin wrote for "A Picture of Her Face,"
a song in waltz time:

This life is very sad to me, a sorrow fills my heart,
My story I will tell you, from me my love did part,

83

The village church bell sadly tolled, the one I loved had died,
She was a treasure more than gold, when she was by my side.
But now she's gone beyond recall, in a silent tomb she sleeps,
The one I loved yet most of all has left me here to weep;
Though death so ruthless stole my love, my dear and only
    Grace,
I've yet a treasure in this world, a picture of her face.

(*Refrain*)

It brings joy to me when ofttimes sad at heart,
Her picture I can see, and sad thoughts then depart;
Although my love is dead, my only darling Grace,
My eyes are ofttimes looking on a picture of her face.[28]

These two songs probably sold modestly well, for it was an era when nearly every parlor had its square or upright piano and sheet music sold for under half a dollar. Piano benches were frequently made large enough to store hundreds of copies of such music. However, these songs of Joplin's could hardly compare to the success of a song like "After the Ball," and perhaps it is best that they did not. For if they had, by circumstance Scott Joplin might have continued writing chiefly in this genre and not ventured as wholeheartedly into instrumental and particularly ragtime composition.

Having published two songs, Joplin was encouraged to compose more works and try to get them in print, and in 1896 he published three compositions in Temple, Texas, once again presumably while with the Texas Medley Quartette in Louisiana and Texas. All three were instrumental works, a waltz and two marches, and their order of publication seems to indicate Joplin's imaginative development and growing boldness. The first to be published was "Harmony Club Waltz," issued by Robert

Smith.[29] Smith also published the second, "Combination March." Both compositions compared favorably with other published marches and waltzes of the time, but, like Joplin's two ballads, they were not particularly distinguished. The third work is different. "Great Crush Collision March," published by John R. Fuller under the agency of Robert Smith, is in some ways a novelty piece, and it may have been intended as such. The sheet music cover contains the blurb, "Dedicated to the M. K. & T. Ry.," (Missouri, Kansas & Texas Railway), and it is possible that a collision had occurred in 1896 in or near Temple, through which the road ran. Joplin may have written the piece under the inspiration of the event; or he may have added sound effects and descriptive narrative to an already completed work to make it timely and cause it to fit the event. It is the first of Joplin's published compositions to contain between-the-lines notes indicating the spirit in which certain passages were to be played—"The noise of the train while running at the rate of sixty miles per hour"; "Whistling for the crossing"; "Noise of the trains"; "Whistle before the collision"; "The collision." Discords become higher and more piercing as they build up to "The collision," which is marked by a crashing fortissimo chord in the base, and in these days when commercial arrangers did not know how to notate anything but regular or "square" meter, such descriptive sections were absolutely necessary. It has been suggested, however, that in his own playing of the composition Joplin would have infused it with considerable syncopation, and that "Great Crush Collision March" is the first publication of Joplin's to contain elements of ragtime.[30]

The Texas Medley Quartette ended this, their last, tour in Joplin, Missouri, in 1897, after which the group disbanded. With Saunders,[31] Scott made his way to Sedalia, which would serve as his base for the next four years. Although he was now a published composer, financially he was not much better off than he had been before his compositions were published. It is unlikely that the terms of his agreements with his publishers included royalties. The common practice among small publishers was to pay twenty-five dollars or fifty dollars outright and acquire all rights to the compositions they purchased. Even if Scott managed to negotiate a contract providing for royalties, his earnings would have been minimal. None of these early works of his were hits, and at the customary 5 per cent royalty rate, many thousands of copies of forty-cent or fifty-cent sheet music would have to be sold to net him more than pin money.

CHAPTER IV

Sedalia

Located near the center of Missouri about one hundred ninety miles west of St. Louis and eighty miles east of Kansas City, Sedalia was not yet forty years old when Scott Joplin arrived. Like many towns, it owed its existence to the railroad. In 1859 General George R. Smith, who had learned that the right of way for the Missouri & Pacific road was projected through the area, had purchased one thousand acres along the surveyed route and marked out the boundaries of a small town amid the rolling prairie hills. He called it Sedville for his daughter Sarah, whom he affectionately called "Sed." Within a few months he had expanded the boundaries and planned a larger town to which he gave the more pleasant-sounding name Sedalia. It was settled in 1860 and the following year the railroad arrived. The town grew quickly after that and by 1895 Sedalia was a prosperous community with a population of some 15,000. It served as the Pettis County seat, the site of the annual Missouri State Fair and a terminal and layover point for not only the Missouri

& Pacific but also the Missouri, Kansas & Texas, the railroad to which Scott had dedicated his "Great Crush Collision March."

During the Civil War, Sedalia had been a Union military post, and this factor, combined with the numerous opportunities for agricultural work and railroad jobs, had attracted a sizable black population. Though blacks were segregated in housing and in social areas (unlike St. Louis directories, the Sedalia city directories identified blacks as "(col)"), the Sedalia black community was more prosperous than that of St. Louis. It supported several newspapers, among them the St. Louis *Palladium*, and boasted the George R. Smith College for Negroes, established by Smith's daughters and later operated by the Methodist Church.

Sedalia also had the distinction of having one of the largest sporting districts in the state. The area, located in the vicinity of Lamine and Main Streets, included more than thirty saloons and attracted a large number of performers, among them Blind Boone, who would offer to pay a thousand dollars cash at his performances to anyone who could play a rag or song that Boone could not duplicate note for note after hearing it just once—and who never had to pay up.[1] Work was plentiful, particularly for those piano players who were facile at playing the new ragtime music, which was already popular in Sedalia and which was beginning to be played in other parts of the country as well.

In January 1897 the first true rag, "Mississippi Rag" had been copyrighted by white Chicago band leader William H. Krell, opening the way for the publication of thousands of others and a nationwide ragtime craze. In Sedalia in 1897 ragtime was still in its infancy, but there were in that one city a group of young men who would become among the most famous ragtime composers and performers. They would soon be joined and personally guided by Scott Joplin. When he arrived, however, Joplin was little more than another black pianist, albeit a published composer with an immersement in his music more singular than that of most others. As Samuel Brunson Campbell, a young white pianist who would arrive in Sedalia in 1899, later wrote, "He liked a little beer, and gambled some, but he never let such things interfere with his music . . . He was then about twenty-nine years old, a very black negro, about five feet seven inches tall; a good dresser, usually neat, but sometimes a little careless with his clothes; gentlemanly and pleasant, with a liking for companionship . . . He and Saunders were inseparable. If one were seen the other wouldn't be far off."[2]

Now that he had been published, Joplin was eager to sell more works. But he realized his notational ability was deficient. Though he could improvise a fine piece of ragtime music on the piano, he had difficulty writing it down. According to Campbell, Joplin was then working at a tavern owned by Tony Williams, a black man who played and taught piano. Williams encouraged Joplin to enroll in the Smith College of Music, part of the George R. Smith College for Negroes on the outskirts of town. Saunders concurred, and shortly thereafter Joplin did take further musical instruction at the college. While studying piano with Mrs. Minnie Jackson and theory and composition with a Professor Murray,[3] he continued setting down on paper his ragtime compositions before he was fully competent to do so. It is likely that he tried to place them with various Sedalia publishers and, finding no success there, journeyed east to Kansas City, where one tune was purchased by music publisher Carl Hoffman. Though it was not published until 1899, "Original Rags" seems an early Joplin composition, written before he had acquired a real facility for notating his music.

The title page of "Original Rags" contained the blurb "Picked by Scott Joplin, Arranged by Chas. N. Daniels." It is the only Joplin publication known whose arrangement is credited to another. Considering that the composition was published in the same year as the famous "Maple Leaf Rag," and is definitely inferior in quality, it is possible that Hoffman purchased the work, held it for a while not knowing quite what to do with it, hired Charles N. Daniels to arrange it,[4] and finally issued it two years later. Though the theory has been advanced that Daniels had simply "arranged to have the piece published," and that Joplin actually did the arrangement himself, it is interesting to note that an article in the St. Louis *Post-Dispatch*, published two years after "Original Rags" was issued, does not mention the composition as one of Joplin's ragtime works.[5]

Its title notwithstanding, "Original Rags" is a simple composition, not a collection. The title probably refers to the fact that it contained several passages played in the new ragged time, a reference that seems to date the composition to a time when the term *rag* was not yet solidified in popular terminology as identifying a single tune. Whether or not Joplin did sell "Original Rags" in 1897, the distinction of being the first black composer to publish a ragtime piece went to his friend, Tom Turpin, whose "Harlem Rag" was published in December 1897.

To support himself while attending the Smith College of Music, Joplin engaged in a variety of musical activities in both the lower-class and better class black Sedalia societies. He joined Sedalia's Queen City Concert Band, an all-black group established in 1891 as the Queen City Negro Band. One of its members was Emmett Cook, who had been a member of the Texas Medley Quartette, and perhaps Cook used his influence to get Joplin into the band. Scott played first B-flat cornet, and under his influence this twelve-piece band became one of the first, if not the first, in the area to play ragtime. In addition, Scott took a nucleus of five pieces from this band—E-flat tuba, baritone cornet, clarinet, drums, and piano—and formed a smaller group to play at parties and dances in the area[6]; not because such activity was particularly enjoyable for him but because there was money in it.[7] Elderly Sedalia residents remember dances given in a building at the present 306–308 West Second Street and at a dance hall then on the northeast corner of Main Street and Ohio Avenue. "It was about the time the cakewalk came out," recalled one such elderly resident, "and Joplin and his friends really made music."[8]

Joplin also worked in the taverns and bawdyhouses of the sporting district. His first steady job was in a white-owned and operated establishment which contained a tavern on the main floor and a gambling parlor on the second. All its customers were white.[9] Later, he played at the Black 400 Club at 108 East Main Street, a club that he frequented as a patron as well.[10] The club, owned and operated probably by W. J. Williams and presided over by C. E. Williams,[11] was also called the 400 Social Club and the 400 Special Club, and it combined elements of both black lowlife and black middle-class life. The cakewalk had been appropriated by whites, and cakewalk music as well as the dance itself had become something of a national craze by 1896, exposing the white general public to syncopated music, deliberately syncopated music, for the first time. Accordingly, the cakewalk had been readopted and refined by blacks. Every summer the Black 400 Club sponsored an all-day outing that featured a picnic, games, and contests, and at the end a grand cakewalk to cap the day's entertainment. S. Brunson Campbell recalled that Joplin claimed he had composed one of the first published cakewalks in honor of this annual event, calling it "The Black 400 Ball."[12]

At the Black 400 Club, where he played primarily for fun, and at the white-owned taverns, where he played chiefly for profit, Scott Joplin impressed his listeners with his perfect pitch, his ability to make ordinary chords and harmonies sound different, his talent at syncopation and rendition of the new ragtime forms. The success of ragtime depended greatly on the quality of its performance, for while its forms indicated the reactions it should inspire, a skilled pianist was necessary to make them a reality, and became more and more necessary as classic ragtime came into being.

A rag's introduction establishes the key of the first large section of the composition and, in its rhythm and tempo, sets the mood. It captures the attention of the listener and lets him know that a rag is beginning to take form. After these first four measures, the opening chorus commands the listener to pay attention by using syncopated elements over a steady base. The second chorus employs a wider range of elements and greater rhythmic complexity, causing the listener's excitement to mount. Then, a calming element is introduced; a bridge acting as the device to reach the more relaxed and melodic third chorus. The next chorus, however, surprises and wakes up the listener. The elemental range is widened once more, it is infused with humor, and it has a "ride-out" quality that signals that the end of the rag is approaching. "It is as though the composer was saying through music—I have excited you, then I allowed you to calm yourself, now have fun—enjoy, for this is ragtime—'sir.'" The fourth chorus ends with a closing section, which unmistakably completes the tune.[13]

Before long, Joplin had attracted a group of talented young followers, among them Joe Jordan, Arthur Marshall, and Scott Hayden. Joe Jordan had been born in 1882 in Cincinnati and had come to Sedalia to hang out in the saloon district and learn from the veteran players. A gifted player himself, he had never had a piano lesson and could not read a note. For this reason, among others, he respected Scott Joplin, and later he took music lessons. "Ear players can't do anything unless they hear it," he used to say. "You can't show them some music and tell them it's going to be a popular song—they have to hear it to play it. How would you like to have the paper read to you all the time to know what's going on?"[14]

Arthur Marshall, born in 1881 in Kansas City, was about sixteen years old when Joplin arrived in Sedalia and was already a musician of considerable talent. He became a classmate of Joplin at the Smith College of Music and before long also became an unofficial student of the older man. Joplin was invited to stay with Marshall in his rooms at 135 West Henry Street and he lived there during most of his Sedalia years.[15] Some seventy-five years later, Marshall would recall their getting together on the "old-time square piano" in his home. "Joplin would say, 'go on, play that piece again, play that piece again,' and we began to get together . . ."[16]

Scott Hayden was about the same age as Arthur Marshall and the two had attended high school together.

Marshall introduced Hayden to Joplin and the three became close friends and musical collaborators. On many a night, the two younger men could be found behind a screen or curtain in the bawdyhouses and saloons where Joplin played, smuggled in by the older man because they were too young to enter by the front door.

Joplin, meanwhile, had completed the first draft of "Maple Leaf Rag," a composition the source of whose title continues to occupy the minds of Joplin scholars. It may have been named simply for the maple tree, one of the most abundant shade trees in Sedalia. It may also have been named after Florence Johnson's "Maple Leaf Waltz," which was popular in Sedalia at the time.[17] The Chicago Great Western Railroad had a route serving Chicago, Kansas City, and Minneapolis-St. Paul known as the Maple Leaf Route, because its route map resembled a maple leaf. Frank W. Cole's 1895 composition "The Maple Leaf Two-Step" had been named for the route.[18] Given Joplin's interest in the railroads, as indicated by "Great Crush Collision March," this route may indeed have been the inspiration for the title of his composition.

At any rate, Joplin was pleased with the composition, his friends liked it, and he felt sure he could sell it. Sometime in 1898 he took it to a Sedalia music publisher, A. W. Perry & Sons, at 360 Broadway, but to his dismay the firm rejected it. A trip to Kansas City and a visit to Carl Hoffman's firm also proved fruitless.[19] His friends encouraged him to continue working on the piece, and he liked it so much that he played it frequently in the clubs where he performed. He was gratified by its reception. Joe Jordan recalled hearing and liking the piece but suggesting to Joplin that he change its key. Originally, Joplin had played it in the key of A, since it was the

94

easiest key for his band, which was composed mostly of A instruments. Jordan suggested that Joplin transpose it to A flat for publication to make it easier to read. Joplin followed Jordan's advice but, Jordan recalled, could not play it in the new key as well as in the original.[20]

Otis Saunders was also convinced of the tune's merit. Not only did he help Joplin rework the composition, but even before it was eventually sold he talked it up, not just in Sedalia but wherever he traveled. In his unpublished autobiography, S. Brunson Campbell explained how he was introduced to Scott Joplin's music: "It was in 1898 that fate introduced me to Negro ragtime. A friend and I ran away to Oklahoma City to a celebration being held there. We became separated and I wandered into the Armstrong-Byrd music store and began to play some of the popular tunes of the day. A crowd gathered to listen, encouraged me with applause and called for more. After a time a young mulatto, light-complexioned, dressed to perfection and smiling pleasantly, came forward. He placed a pen-and-ink manuscript of music in front of me entitled 'Maple Leaf Rag,' by Scott Joplin. I played it and he seemed impressed. (He afterwards told me I had made two mistakes.) He turned out to be Otis Saunders, a fine pianist and ragtime composer, a pal of Scott Joplin and one of ragtime's first pioneers. I learned from him that Joplin was then living in Sedalia and that he, Saunders, was joining him there in a few days." Although he did not mention it to Saunders, Campbell was already making up his mind to go to Sedalia, too.

In December of 1898 the Maple Leaf Club applied for official legal status as an organization. The "Articles of Agreement for the Maple Leaf Club of Sedalia, Missouri," dated December 23, 1898, read in part: "The objects and purposes for which this organization is created is to form and maintain a club, and to maintain a club house for the purpose of advancing by social intercourse the bodily and mental health of such persons as might be or hereafter become its members, and by the friendly interchange of views and discussions, advance the interests of its members; to obtain a place of common and friendly intercourse of such members with each other, to maintain a library for its members, other spheres of amusement and entertainments for the benefit of its members." The board of directors for the club's first year were: H. L. Dixon, President; Thomas Tompkins, Vice-President; A. E. Ellis, Secretary; W. J. Williams, Treasurer; and W. B. Williams. Among the first thirty members were Scott Joplin and Arthur Marshall.[21]

Although Joplin's "Maple Leaf Rag" was not yet either purchased or published, it is possible that the Maple Leaf Club was named for the work. As stated earlier, the composition was popular in Sedalia before it was accepted for publication. However, it is also possible that "Maple Leaf Rag" was named for the club, which could have been in existence in some form for some time before official recognition was sought.[22] Indeed, a charter may have been applied for to allay criticism of the club. On January 18, 1899, the Sedalia *Democrat* published the following item:

The Colored ministers of the city have made request of the city officials that the Black 400 Social Club and the Maple Leaf Club be closed. 'By permanently putting an end to these abominable loafing places—hot beds of immorality you will stop a great source of vice, create a better moral atmosphere for our young people, and render some of our homes happier.'

There was no rebuttal from the Maple Leaf Club, but C. E. Williams, president of the Black 400 Club, requested space for this statement in response:

> That the Black 400 club room is a den of immorality is not true, and no eyewitness will say so. At the dress balls 40 of the best white people of Sedalia were in attendance as spectators . . . The doors of the club room are always open for the admission of the officers of the city to see what is going on.[23]

Apparently, the black ministers' appeal went unheeded. The February 15, 1899, issue of the *Democrat* contained the report: "The Black 400 gave a Valentine ball last night and the Maple Leaf Club also kept open house."[24]

Besides being a charter member, Scott Joplin also became resident pianist at the Maple Leaf Club, and naturally "Maple Leaf Rag" was his most popular number. In club publicity he was called "the entertainer," as the blurb on the back of a club business card shows. The front of the card read simply: "The Maple Leaf Club, Sedalia, Mo. 121 East Main St., W. J. Williams, Prop." On the back was printed the following:

The Good Time Boys

William's Place, for Williams, E. Cook, Allie Ellis, Taylor Williams. Will give a good time, for instance Master Scott Joplin, the entertainer. W. J. Williams, the slow wonder said that H. L. Dixon, the crackerjack around ladies said E. Cook, the ladies masher told Dan Smith, the clever boy, he saw Len Williams, the dude, and he said that there are others but not so good. These are the members of the "Maple Leaf Club."[25]

One twenty-one East Main Street was a wooden building on whose ground floor was located the Blocher Seed Store.[26] The Maple Leaf Club was on the second floor, equipped with a large bar and probably filled with pool and gaming tables. Hanging gas lamps situated over the bar and tables scarcely illuminated the piano in the far corner, and the smoke and sounds of conversation often obscured the view and the sound of the ordinary performer. But not on a night when Scott Joplin was there. Decades later, at the age of eighty-eight, Arthur Marshall would recall how the rafters shook when "Scott took the stool at the ole '88 in the Maple Leaf."[27] Tom Turpin would come to the club on his visits to Sedalia, and nearly every itinerant pianist made it a point to go to the Maple Leaf Club to hear Joplin while he was in town.

"Original Rags" was published early in 1899. Joplin could not have been very pleased with the cover, which showed an old "darkie" picking up rags in front of a tumbledown shack. It was the type of "coon cover" that was popular at the time, and Joplin probably understood that Hoffman's cover choice was simply in the current vogue. "Original Rags" was not of much concern to Joplin, however, for though it was his first published rag already he had developed far beyond it. His "Maple Leaf Rag" was, in his opinion, a fine composition. On the advice of his friends he had reworked it into what he felt was a highly salable piece.

While reworking "Maple Leaf Rag," Joplin was working with his protégés Arthur Marshall and Scott Hayden on what would be called "Swipesy—Cake Walk" and "Sunflower Slow Drag—A Ragtime Two-Step" respectively. Of the two, the Hayden collaboration progressed more quickly, for Joplin was attracted to Hayden's young widowed sister Belle. He was a shy man, and not one to declare himself openly, and thus he used the collaborative effort as an excuse to spend a considerable amount of time at the Haydens' rooms on 133 West Cooper. Joplin took the manuscript for "Sunflower" along with a re-worked version of "Maple Leaf Rag" when he visited the offices of John Stark, located at that time at 114 East Fifth Street in Sedalia in the summer of 1899. He had not gone to Stark earlier because the company published pri-marily sentimental parlor piano music. That Joplin did eventually go to Stark and that the publisher discerned the potential in the music he offered is one of the happy events of history.

John Stark was born in Shelby County, Kentucky, in 1841, and had left home when the Civil War broke out, becoming a bugler in the Indiana Heavy Artillery Volun-teers. After the war, he and his bride set out in a covered wagon to homestead in the area of Maryville, Missouri. Finding the life of a homesteader not to his liking, Stark eventually turned to selling musical instruments. In 1883 he moved to Sedalia and established a music shop at 222 Ohio Street, where he concentrated on selling pianos and organs. "They used to drag an organ out to a farmer's house in an old wagon and leave it there for a week," the widow of Stark's son, Will, recalled years later. "When they came back, the farmer invariably had become so at-tached to the instrument, that he would buy it."[28]

In 1885, at the age of forty-four, he established his sheet music business, John Stark & Son, with one of his sons, Will. It was a modest enterprise. The two men oper-ated their one handpress themselves and worked not in business suits but in overalls. And the composers whose work they published were frequently friends and members of the family, among them John Stark's son E. J. (Etilmon Justice), who composed typical nineteenth-century parlor music before the ragtime craze and who later published rags under the name Bud Manchester. A number of the early Stark publications were actually E. J. Stark's pieces published under pseudonyms.[29] Works by other composers were usually purchased for little money, often only a small percentage of the royalties and no outright purchase amount, and because they operated on a shoestring the Starks favored "safe" pieces and took few risks on music that they were not sure would sell. It took a talent like that of Scott Joplin to cause them to change their policy.

Scott Joplin entered the Stark establishment one day in August 1899, carrying the manuscripts for "Maple Leaf Rag" and "Sunflower Slow Drag" and accompanied by a small boy who had probably been conscripted for the occasion. Dance being the basis of ragtime, Joplin may have realized that a demonstration of the "danceability" of his compositions would make them more salable. As Joplin played "Maple Leaf Rag" and then "Sunflower Slow Drag," the little boy did a dance, impressing both Stark and son. Although the elder Stark was apprehensive, feeling the compositions were too difficult for the average person to play, Will Stark was so taken by the child's dance that he decided to buy at least one of the compositions and accepted "Maple Leaf Rag,"[30] beginning one of the legendary relationships in American music history. In the years to come, though they had differences, Stark, the white businessman, and Joplin, the black composer, dealt with each other from positions of mutual respect, a remarkable relationship for the times.

On August 10, 1899, John Stark and Scott Joplin signed a contract setting forth the terms under which the firm would publish "Maple Leaf Rag." Scott received no money up front and he was to receive a royalty of only one cent per copy sold.[31] But he was intent on having his work published and willing to agree to almost any terms. In fact, so great was his desire to see his work published that he was shortly to sign an exclusive five-year contract with John Stark & Son.[32]

This, in itself, was quite a remarkable event. At the time it was not common to publish works by black composers, and those whose works were published were frequently exploited. White publishers could purchase a tune or song for ten dollars and reap a considerable profit. The hapless composers would take anything to see their work in print. John Stark was not above such exploitation, as the contract for "Maple Leaf Rag" indicates; yet he was remembered with fondness by black composers of the era and regarded as a pioneer for purchasing rags in the early years of ragtime. "John Stark was a very far-sighted man," Joe Jordan once observed. "Nobody would publish rags in the early years." Jordan sold his biggest hit, "That Teasin' Rag," for twenty-five dollars. ("I thought I was holding the man up!") Later Stark purchased many rags for twenty-five or fifty dollars, and these were large sums for itinerant composers.[33]

"Maple Leaf Rag" was published in September 1899. The actual music was printed in St. Louis, but it is still called the Sedalia Edition.[34] Its cover was far more tastefully done than that of "Original Rags," and this would be one characteristic of the Starks' business that would please Joplin. While their covers would be designed for salability, they would not be exploitative. In fact, the cover illustration for "Maple Leaf Rag" was the most exploitative of any of Joplin's works published by John Stark & Son. It depicts two black couples in decorous dress as if engaged in or on their way to a cakewalk, an illustration not originated in the Stark minds but used by permission of the American Tobacco Company, which employed it in their advertising for Old Virginia Sheroots. The Stark firm was not large enough to commission original covers at that time. Clearly, the use of the cakewalk association was to take advantage of the current cakewalk craze. Unfortunately, the cover had not the desired effect. "Maple Leaf Rag" was hardly a smash hit at first. As John Stark later said, ". . . it took us one year to sell 400 copies, simply because people examined it hastily, and didn't find it."[35]

The reference is probably to the lilting tune. In those days before radio and phonograph, far more people were able to read music than today. Likely, they skimmed the notes and either decided the tune was too difficult or did not discern its charm. What would eventually sell "Maple Leaf Rag" was word-of-mouth advertising, hearing the piece played in music shops and in saloons and taverns. But at first it was a slow seller, and at fifty cents a copy it was not making either publisher or composer rich. At one-cent royalty per copy, Scott Joplin made exactly four dollars in the first year after the piece was published, hardly a big score. He still had to perform in a variety of capacities in order to support himself and he and his band were in considerable demand to play at community functions. The Sedalia *Democrat*, August 4, 1899, carried the following in an article about the Celebration of Emancipation Day at Liberty Park:

Fourth of August Musicale—Scott Joplin, assisted by John Williams, Lynn Williams, Frank Bledsoe, Arthur Channel and Richard Smith, will render the programme.

He also continued to play at the Maple Leaf Club, where in 1899, fifteen-year-old Samuel Brunson Campbell found him.

As Campbell later wrote, in his autobiography, "I headed for Sedalia and after riding in box cars, cattle cars, and 'blind baggage,' I finally reached there and lost no time seeking out Otis Saunders and Scott Joplin . . . At Saunders' request I played for Joplin. They both thought I played fine piano and Joplin agreed to teach me his style of ragtime. He taught me how to play his first four rags, the 'Original Rags,' 'Maple Leaf Rag,' 'Sunflower Slow Drag,' and 'Swipesey Cake Walk.' I was the first white pianist to play and master his famous 'Maple Leaf.'"

To be sure, ragtime in general and "Maple Leaf Rag" in particular took some mastering. In typical ragtime form, it consisted of four different tunes or strains, each sixteen bars long. The first strain was sophisticated in its harmony, pleasing in its perfection. The second strain was in a "dance" style, similar to that in "Original Rags." The third strain was the one now most featured and frequently played, because of its exciting march rhythm and its pounding agitation. Unlike Joplin's later compositions, it could be played extremely fast without detracting from it, and in fact could not be played slowly and retain its lightness. There was a happy feeling about it, and an impulse to dance that was irresistible. But it had to be played properly for this impulse to be transmitted. The

Starks acknowledged this difficulty in one of their later advertisements:

> We knew a pianist who had in her repertoire, "The Maple Leaf," "Sunflower Slow Drag," "The Entertainer" and "Elite Syncopations." She had played them as she thought, over and over for her own pleasure and others, until at last she had laid them aside as *passé*. But it chanced that she incidentally dropped into a store one day, where Joplin was playing "The Sunflower Slow Drag." She was instantly struck with its unique and soulful story, and—what do you think? She asked someone what it was. She had played over it and around it for twelve months and had never touched it.[36]

Many who tried to play ragtime from sheet music *played* it less than they played *at* it, and quite a few didn't even try. This was one reason why "Maple Leaf Rag" did not sell well at first. Another reason was that ragtime had not yet become a national craze. To many, perhaps the majority of Americans, it was still associated with lowlife Negroes and red-light districts and was hardly entertainment suitable for polite society.

Scott Joplin was deeply aware of this attitude and pained by it. More than anything else, he wanted so-called Negro music to be respectable, understood for its possibilities, seen for what it was, not burdened with negative associations. "As early as the turn of the century," Campbell would recall much later, "Joplin had the idea that his fine ragtime music could stand up with the best of the so-called 'better music.' . . . He thought his music unappreciated and once said, 'Maybe fifty years after I am dead it will be.'"[37]

Joplin was determined to win respectability for rag-

time. For some months before "Maple Leaf Rag" was published he had been at work on a piece unheard of for the time, a dramatic ragtime folk ballet. Based on black social dances of the era, *The Ragtime Dance* consisted of a vocal introduction followed by a series of dance themes directed by the vocalist: Ragtime Dance, Clean Up Dance, Jennie Cooks Dance, Slow Drag, World's Fair Dance, Back Step Prance, Dude Walk, Sedidus Walk, Town Talk, and Stop Time. In retrospect, it can be seen as a logical early step in Joplin's development toward full-length opera. But in the fall of 1899 it was a rather strange and somewhat pretentious undertaking for a man who had published relatively few compositions and only two ragtime compositions, none of which had sold particularly well as yet, despite the local popularity of the "Maple Leaf Rag." And it was highly pretentious for a black man.

Scott Joplin, however, was not a practical man. His desire to make ragtime music respectable outweighed any misgivings he might have had about the reception of his folk ballet. And perhaps his popularity in and around Sedalia—the sheer idolatry with which his young protégés viewed him—clouded his vision. They praised his work, helped him with it; Arthur Marshall spent weeks copying in longhand the many parts of the orchestration. Joplin's brother Will encouraged him. It is understandable that for a brief, heady time Scott Joplin thought he might be able to influence the path of ragtime and change the predominant attitude about Negro music.

Joplin formed the Scott Joplin Drama Company, whose members included Will Joplin and Henry Jackson, with whom Scott would later collaborate on a song.[38] Late in 1899 he rented the Woods Opera House in Sedalia for a

single performance, which he hoped would be sufficient to arouse excitement about the composition, for a single performance was all he could afford. He invited nearly everyone he knew, including the Stark family, and no doubt let it be known to the others that a favorable reception to the piece might influence the Starks to purchase the ballet for publication.

The curtain went up. In the orchestra pit below, Scott Joplin on piano conducted the small orchestra that was the nucleus of the Queen City Concert Band. On stage, before a simple scenery backdrop, Will Joplin sang his introduction, then acted as a caller as four couples dressed in their own most festive clothing danced the various steps. When it was over, the audience applauded heartily, but John Stark was not moved to purchase the composition. "Maple Leaf Rag," after all, had not been out long and had not begun to sell at any great pace. This was an ambitious undertaking and Stark was too good a businessman to take such a gamble. In his opinion Joplin had not yet proved the marketability of his works, and this was far from the ordinary rag anyway. In retrospect, Joplin showed bad timing; but even if he had waited until "Maple Leaf Rag" had really begun to sell he probably would not have been successful in convincing Stark to publish *The Ragtime Dance*. It was too far ahead of its time. Even so, Joplin blamed John Stark for his lack of foresight. The matter of *The Ragtime Dance* would linger in the background of their relationship and cloud it for some years to come.

Though Joplin was disappointed at Stark's failure to purchase his ragtime ballet, he remained undaunted in his intention to keep setting down his ragtime compositions. They came easily to him, and with his training at

the Smith College of Music they became increasingly easy to set down. Then, too, he was buoyed by the support and encouragement of his friends and protégés, who were constantly helping to spread his music and his name around Sedalia and its environs. One of these protégés was Samuel Brunson Campbell, who late in 1899 announced that he was leaving Sedalia. He wanted to return home to his family in Kansas, but everywhere he went, he informed his idol, he would play Scott Joplin's rags. Just before he left, Campbell had an encounter with Joplin: "As I was leaving him and Sedalia to return to my home in Kansas he gave me a bright, new shiny half dollar and called my attention to the date on it. 'Kid,' he said, 'this half dollar is dated 1897, the year I wrote my first rag. Carry it for good luck and as you go through life it will always be a reminder of your early ragtime days here at Sedalia.' There was a strange look in his eyes which I shall never forget."[39]

Scott Joplin, too, would always remember his days in Sedalia, for there he was the acknowledged "King of Ragtime" and was indeed referred to by that title. He had the city by its nose. He took, for example, to organizing ragtime playing contests, and performers from all over the state would come to compete with him. Many, especially those from St. Louis and Kansas City, were accompanied by rooting sections, but all the Sedalia people would favor Joplin. When it came time to choose the winner for the contest, he would always win by acclaim.

His name and his music were being spread at the same time in the other towns and cities throughout the Midwest by Samuel Brunson Campbell in Missouri, Kansas, and Nebraska and by Otis Saunders in Oklahoma City and Memphis. And Scott Joplin, too, traveled away from Sedalia at times, playing for college students and performing at least once in Warrensburg, Missouri. In some of the communities he visited, Maple Leaf Clubs were formed.[40]

By 1900 ragtime was becoming a national craze, and in fact it would give the new decade its popular name, the "Gay Nineties." One reason for its popularity was the "amateur music movement." In the decades since the Civil War the parlor piano had become the mainstay of American middle-class culture, and thus a music specifically or primarily for the piano was almost assured of popularity. But two other elements were important to the success of ragtime music. One was the emergence of the commercial music market as a major cultural force. Based in New York, this mass music market very shortly began to demand the new ragtime but in simpler form, and New York-based composers and musicians quickly created the supply to meet the demand. Beginning about 1900, these composers and musicians supplied the numerous New York music publishing firms with pieces marked by the syncopation of classic ragtime (classic ragtime is defined very simply by most musicologists as the music of Scott Joplin, James Scott, Joseph Lamb) but far simpler to play and much more commercialized. Their "tinny" sound gave rise to the name Tin Pan Alley, which the world of the New York-based ragtime musicians was called. True to the history of American music, these commercialists of ragtime were primarily white, had adopted and adapted a chiefly black musical idiom, and were now busily engaged in popularizing it.

The other element was the perfection of the Pianola, forerunner of the player piano, a mechanism that enabled the piano to be played mechanically. A paper roll was passed over a cylinder containing apertures connected to tubes, which were in turn connected to the piano action. As often as a hole in the paper passed over an aperture, a current of air passed through a tube and caused the corresponding hammer to strike the string. The performances of the finest pianists could be reproduced with some skill. With the emergence in the United States of a strong middle class, the attitude that with enough money the proper results could be achieved had begun to prevail. Time is money, and if a middle-class family could afford a Pianola and piano rolls, then they did not have to waste time learning to play on a standard piano the tunes they wanted to waft through their front parlor. A lot of poor, commercialized ragtime was beginning to be published in both piano roll and sheet music form, but it did not overshadow the more classic ragtime compositions. There was plenty of business to go around.

John Stark was convinced that "Maple Leaf Rag" could take advantage of this growing popularity, but he felt handicapped in Sedalia. He needed to be based in a larger city, and late in 1900 he and his son Will journeyed to St. Louis because, as Will Stark's widow later recalled, "they thought they would have a better chance of putting it over here." They set up shop in their hotel room and, operating a small handpress, turned out some ten thousand copies of "Maple Leaf Rag," which they traded for a small printing plant at 3615 Laclede Avenue.[41]

John Stark & Son was still very much a one-horse operation, and in fact operated a tuning business during the first two years or so in St. Louis.[42] Wishing to establish themselves as a bona fide St. Louis publishing firm, the Starks made haste to issue a new title and chose "Swipesy —Cake Walk," the Joplin-Marshall collaboration. Pub-

lished at the end of 1900, the first Stark publication to
bear the St. Louis address, "Swipesy—Cake Walk" is also
the first true *slow* drag, as the instructions on the first
page—"Slow"—indicate. Its variations of speed are meant
to conform to similar variations in the dance that was the
current rage, and it was specifically titled a cakewalk. Although it has not the imaginative flair of "Maple Leaf
Rag," it is a respectable work and does not deserve some
of the criticism it has received from musicologists who
feel that it is primarily a Marshall composition with a few
Joplin strains inserted rather than a real co-operative
effort.[43]

Stark designed his own cover for this composition, and
though it depicts a small Negro boy it is done tastefully.
According to legend Stark discovered the little newsboy
squabbling out in front of his office one day, was taken
with him, and decided to bring him in and have him pho-
tographed for the cover of the new composition. Looking
at the photograph, Stark decided the boy's shy expression
was that of a child who had just been into the cookie jar.
"Let's call it Swipesy," Stark said, and thus was the title of
the composition born.[44] Many rag titles came about in just
such a casual manner.

The little boy's photograph was not the only one to
grace the sheet music cover. Below him were two smaller
photographs of the collaborative composers, the first and
one of the few published photographs of Scott Joplin, a
solemn-looking man in a three-piece suit, his stiff pose
resembling that in a front-view police mug shot. Perhaps
he was concerned that the public would be less likely to
buy a composition whose writers were clearly identified as
a black. Many black composers were aware that the pub-

lic purchased their compositions thinking they were written by whites.

Sometime in the fall of 1900 "Maple Leaf Rag" suddenly took off. A flood of orders came in, many of them—perhaps the largest number—from the F. W. Woolworth five-and-ten-cent stores, and John Stark & Son was barely equipped to handle them. Shortly they hired a staff, exchanged their work clothes for business suits, and set up an operation more in keeping with the sort associated with the publishers of a work like "Maple Leaf Rag."[45]

The St. Louis edition of "Maple Leaf Rag" had a different and considerably less interesting cover. In the spring of 1901 the cheroot business of the American Tobacco Company was transferred to American Cigar Company,[46] who apparently refused to allow further use of their illustration by the Starks. A cover illustration showing a simple maple leaf was substituted.

Back in Sedalia, Scott Joplin continued his composing and his performing at the Maple Leaf Club. While he was considering moving to St. Louis, there were things that held him back. One was his disagreement with Stark over the marketability of *The Ragtime Dance*. Joplin wanted the work published, and after Stark left Sedalia, the composer visited other publishers in the city trying to sell the work. While he was unsuccessful in selling *The Ragtime Dance,* he did manage to sell another rag, "The Favorite," to A. W. Perry & Sons of Sedalia.[47] Clearly, Joplin was angry at Stark for not seeing the possibilities in *The Ragtime Dance* and thus did not feel totally obligated to the five-year contract between the two. Yet he did not wish to lose Stark's friendship or his publishing business altogether. It is likely that he secured an agreement from Perry not to publish "The Favorite" until 1904, when the five-year contract, entered into in 1899, would be finished.

Then, too, Joplin was courting Belle Hayden and did not wish to leave her. By most accounts, Belle loved Joplin but was not in the least interested in music—his or anyone else's. She would thus not have been particularly understanding of the reason for the move and would have preferred not to leave her family and friends. Sometime in late 1900 or early 1901, however, Joplin met a man from St. Louis who would have a strong effect on him and on his music and whose presence in St. Louis would make it even more important to Joplin to be there too. This man was none other than the legendary German music teacher whose identity would subsequently be one of the unsolved mysteries in the search for material on Joplin's life. Joplin's widow, Lottie, recalled after his death that there had been a German music teacher to whom her husband was indebted and to whom he sent letters and gifts after they had moved to New York. There can be little doubt that Alfred Ernst was this man. This author discovered the man's identity by accident, while searching for suitable illustrations for this book.

The February 28, 1901, issue of the white St. Louis *Post-Dispatch* carried an article that departed from the paper's usual type of reportage. Under the headline "To Play Ragtime in Europe" was a photograph of Scott Joplin, black ragtime musician. The article read:

> Director Alfred Ernst of the St. Louis Choral Symphony Society believes that he has discovered, in Scott Joplin of Sedalia, a negro, an extraordinary genius as a composer of ragtime music.
>
> So deeply is Mr. Ernst impressed with the ability of the

Sedalian that he intends to take with him to Germany next summer copies of Joplin's work, with a view to educating the dignified disciples of Wagner, Liszt, Mendelssohn and other European masters of music into an appreciation of the real American ragtime melodies. It is possible that the colored man may accompany the distinguished conductor.

When he returns from the storied Rhine Mr. Ernst will take Joplin under his care and instruct him in the theory and harmony of music.

Joplin has published two ragtime pieces, "Maple Leaf Rag" and "Swipesey Cake Walk," which will be introduced in Germany by the St. Louis musician.

"I am deeply interested in this man," said Mr. Ernst to the Post-Dispatch. "He is young and undoubtedly has a fine future. With proper cultivation, I believe, his talent will develop into positive genius. Being of African blood himself, Joplin has a keener insight into that peculiar branch of melody than white composers. His ear is particularly acute.

"Recently I played for him portions of 'Tannhauser.' He was enraptured. I could see that he comprehended and appreciated this class of music. It was the opening of a new world to him, and I believe he felt as Keats felt when he first read Chapman's Homer.

"The work Joplin has done in ragtime is so original, so distinctly individual, and so melodious withal, that I am led to believe he can do something fine in compositions of a higher class when he shall have been instructed in theory and harmony.

"Joplin's work, as yet, has a certain crudeness, due to his lack of musical concatenation, but it shows that the soul of the composer is there and needs but to be set free by knowledge of technique. He is an unusually intelligent young man and fairly well educated."

Joplin is known in Sedalia as "The Ragtime King." A trip to Europe in company with Prof. Ernst is the dream of his life. It may be realized.

This was the first of only a few articles that would ever publicly recognize and laud Joplin's talent during his lifetime. To be praised in such a way was to be accorded an honor known by few other black musicians of the era, an honor Scott Joplin had never before experienced and would experience pitifully few times. Like his relationship with Stark, his relationship with Ernst would be quite singular for the era. He would be indebted to Ernst for the rest of his life, and as a result of Ernst's influence, he would aspire to achievements few other black musicians would dare consider: he would presume to write ragtime opera.

The reasons for making the move from Sedalia to St. Louis now far outweighed any reasons against doing so, and sometime probably in the early spring of 1901 Scott Joplin and Belle Hayden left Sedalia to settle in the Gateway City.[48]

CHAPTER V

St. Louis

Arriving in St. Louis, Scott and Belle moved into a second-floor flat in a row house at 2658-A Morgan Town Road,[1] and in keeping with his new domestic status Scott began a more settled life, performing only rarely and concentrating on composing and teaching. He listed himself in the city directory as simply "Joplin, Scott, music." Now that he was in the same city with his mentor, he spent considerable time with Ernst, who would shortly leave for Europe. Although there is no documentary evidence regarding Joplin's whereabouts in the summer of 1901, it is unlikely that he accompanied Ernst, as the St. Louis *Post-Dispatch* hinted he might.[2] He and Belle had moved to St. Louis so recently and their financial condition was probably too modest for such an extravagance. Then, too, Ernst may have wished to introduce Joplin's music to his countrymen before introducing them to its composer. Joplin probably remained in St. Louis that summer.

Not long after the Joplins arrived in the city, Scott Hayden followed them with his bride, Nora Wright, whom he had married in Sedalia. The couple also moved into the house on Morgan Town Road. Arthur Marshall had gone on tour with McCabe's Minstrels, a popular group at the time, but other Sedalians, among them Otis Saunders, would visit frequently. In some ways it was as if an important segment of the Sedalia musical world had simply been transplanted to St. Louis. Certainly, Belle enjoyed these visitors and their news from home, and she later became closer than ever to Arthur Marshall, for one, although she still did not share or understand their interest in music.

For Scott, moving to St. Louis was like coming home. His younger brother Robert was living in the city, in rooms at 2617 Lawton Street, working as a cook. He had stayed in Texarkana and married, and with his wife Cora he'd had a daughter, Essie. But the marriage had failed, and although he was not as musically talented as his brothers, Robert enjoyed the excitement of the big city musical world. Perhaps as a result of Scott's reports of this excitement in his letters home, Robert had decided to move to St. Louis and try to make a new beginning. Within the next year, Will Joplin would also move to St. Louis, taking rooms in a large rooming house at 2117 Lucas Avenue and listing himself in the 1902 city directory as "Joplin, William, music." Once again, a segment of the Joplin family would be together.

And then there were the Turpins, with whom Scott had been so close during his earlier stay in St. Louis. Since Joplin had left St. Louis around 1896, the Turpins' fortunes had risen and fallen with the speed of a roller coaster. Tom's cafe, established in late 1894–early 1895 after his father's Silver Dollar Saloon had closed, had itself folded within a year and Tom had been forced to work as a laborer. By all accounts, with his rugged physique—he is said to have weighed 360 pounds—and huge, meaty hands he looked more like a laborer than a composer-musician anyway. He had continued to work on his music and in late 1895, inspired by a trip to New York, had written his "Harlem Rag," which he sold to DeYoung of St. Louis. Issued in 1897, "Harlem Rag" was the first rag by a black composer to be published, and it would become a minor classic. DeYoung later sold the piece to Stern of New York, which printed it in two different arrangements.[3]

With the money and the optimism gained from the publication of his first rag, Turpin had opened another saloon at 100 N. Nineteenth Street, but this, too, had lasted only about a year. Another trip to New York, where a dance called the Buck and Wing was the rage, inspired his second published rag, "Bowery Buck," issued in 1899. For a time around 1899, Tom Turpin had exchanged the insecure life of a saloonkeeper for the steady income of a police constable, but he had soon decided against such a career, preferring instead to work at menial jobs while pursuing his music,[4] while his father, John, operated yet another saloon.[5]

When Scott Joplin arrived in St. Louis, Tom Turpin was teaching music and functioning as a mentor to a number of talented youngsters, among them Joe Jordan, who had come from Sedalia a year or so before, Sam Patterson, and Louis Chauvin. All were in their late teens or early twenties, and all were seasoned performers. Chauvin and Patterson, seventeen and nineteen respectively in 1900, had been born next door to one another in St. Louis and had attended elementary and junior high schools together. Both had displayed early musical talent, and while Patterson had been given the benefit of lessons and Chauvin had not, Patterson always maintained that Chauvin was the more gifted player. Patterson had dropped out of school at the age of fifteen and Chauvin had quit too. He was thirteen at the time. That summer they went on the road with a company called the Alabama Jubilee Singers. Back in St. Louis, they formed a vocal quartet, the Mozart Comedy Four, and played the city's red-light district as well as gigs in surrounding towns. They also continued to do piano performances. Whenever they were not working they could be found with Tom Turpin, picking up pointers on playing technique. Turpin's technical brilliance was acknowledged throughout the district, although Charlie Thompson, who arrived in St. Louis around 1907, used to say he got more credit than he deserved because he was Scott Joplin's "runnin' buddy."[8] They also exchanged ideas with Turpin. Chauvin was himself a talented composer, but he rarely perfected one strain or harmony before he was off on another. Turpin tried to persuade him to slow down and to think seriously about getting his work published, but Chauvin was unable to concentrate on any one tune for that long.

The interest in Joplin on the part of Alfred Ernst did not cause the composer to forsake his earlier friends of the red-light milieu. He rejoined the Turpin circle and was welcomed with great delight and pride. His "Maple Leaf Rag" was fast making him the most famous rag composer on the circuit, and in the early spring of 1901 three more tunes were added to his list of published works. The compositions, "Sunflower Slow Drag," "Peacherine Rag," and "Augustan Club Waltz," had all been in Stark's possession for some time. "Sunflower Slow Drag," on which Joplin had collaborated with Hayden, was the other composition that Joplin had taken with him on his first visit to the Stark offices in Sedalia. The delay in publishing these new works had been due to the tremendous popularity of "Maple Leaf Rag" and the initial unpreparedness of the Stark firm to fill all the orders that came in. Enlisting the help of every member of the family as well as that of paid employees, the Starks had finally caught up with the backlog of orders and established facilities equipped to handle their mushrooming business, so that by early 1901 they were able to consider publishing new compositions. Encouraged by Joplin's frequent reminders that they had new material of his that they were supposed to publish, and envisioning the coattail effect "Maple Leaf Rag" would have on sales of these new works, John Stark was just as eager to issue them as Joplin was to see them in print.

Probably "Sunflower Slow Drag" and "Augustan Club Waltz" were issued almost simultaneously, for each cover lists the other among Joplin's earlier compositions. "Augustan Club Waltz," dedicated "To the Augustan Club, Sedalia, Mo.," is a typical waltz in the waltz tradition and is in no way a ragtime waltz. And yet it has a hint of Joplin-type ragtime charm, and some have identified elements of its second strain with his later composition, "The Entertainer."

"Sunflower Slow Drag," is in the cakewalk style of ragtime, and it is a truly inspired composition. Perhaps, as John Stark suggested in his advertisement, this inspiration came from Joplin's courtship with Belle Hayden. Stark called it "a song without words," and there are sections for which this is a perfect description.

It is likely that "Peacherine Rag" came later in the

year. It is the first whose cover boldly proclaims, "By the King of Ragtime Writers, Scott Joplin," and it lists the four other Stark-published compositions. Not particularly distinguished, it would nevertheless sell well, and thenceforth Joplin would be known by that proud title.

That title would prove to have disadvantages, however. Despite the fact that it placed Joplin at the head of ragtime *writers*, not performers, there were those who viewed him much as, out West, young men looked upon well-known gunfighters. Their goal was a showdown. By the time Scott Joplin returned, the style of ragtime playing in St. Louis had changed. Gradually, the heavy march two-beat, the oom-pah of the left hand, had disappeared and been replaced by four evenly accented beats in the same interval. At the same time, right-hand play had become more complicated in its accenting. It was a speedier, more infectious type of playing, and those who were good at it viewed as inferior performers those who could not. Tom Turpin, Sam Patterson, Joe Jordan, and most of the others who frequented the district favored the faster style. Only Louis Chauvin preferred the older tempos.

A popular pastime among musicians in the district was "cutting contests," in which two pianists vied with each other to play faster and more varied versions of the same tune. There was no quicker path to acceptance for a young newcomer than to get the best of a veteran of the district in a cutting contest. As soon as word got around that Scott Joplin was in town, many piano players were anxious to challenge him to cutting contests, and at first he complied. "Every time he sat down at the piano he played 'Maple Leaf Rag,'" Charlie Thompson once said. Nor did Joe Jordan ever remember hearing Joplin play any but his own compositions, and Jordan remembers that Joplin played them almost exactly as they were written in sheet music form.[7] When he found that many of his listeners favored the new style and considered his style heavy and plodding, Scott refused further competition, no doubt sadly remembering the Sedalia days when he won every ragtime playing contest. Undaunted, the challengers would pretend real interest in one of his compositions and after persuading him to play it, would sit down at the piano and play their own variations of his work at lightning speed. Though men like Tom Turpin and Louis Chauvin, secure in their own talent, did not feel the need to build themselves up by breaking others down and remained his steadfast supporters, Joplin was deeply affected by these experiences. His visits to the musicians' hangouts in the district became less frequent, and when he did appear he refused to go near the piano. Though the sporting life had never been comfortable for him and though he was happier living his quiet life composing and teaching and learning from Ernst, Joplin had been a performer for too many years not to miss playing for a crowd. But he had tremendous pride, and he would not play for people who did not understand his style.

This is not to say that Joplin fell from favor in St. Louis. He was a published composer and much respected. Most in the district stood by him. And though his rags were slower and more serious than others, many appreciated their musical value and even two-stepped to them.

There were two traditions in ragtime, the composing tradition and the performing tradition, and very few people managed to straddle the line between the two, for they required radically different temperaments. The performing tradition emphasized the moment, the one-shot improvisation, the transitory joy of an exciting variation that would never be played quite the same way again. A tradition that would reach its height in New York's Tin Pan Alley, it was associated with all the lowlife images of the sporting district, and with some reason. That was an underground, bohemian life, an escape from the prejudices of the larger society to be sure, but in its own way a trap. It was a fast-paced life, stimulated by drink and drugs. People died of drug overdose, of syphilis—deaths in the early twenties were not uncommon for this subculture—and once you got in, you rarely had the opportunity to get out.

The other tradition, the composing tradition, was the more attractive, even to the performers. If you could write, then getting your work published was the name of the game. And if you were black and published, you were particularly admired. Even those who delighted in "cutting" Scott Joplin would have preferred to have half his compositional talent. Jelly Roll Morton, for example, became famous for his "left-hand" piano playing, for his prowess in the new style of performance. Charlie Thompson remembers that when Jelly Roll visited St. Louis he delighted in showing off his talent. A short man, he would rear himself up to his full height as someone else played. Then, when the performance was over he would say, "Now let me show you how that piece is supposed to go."[8] Yet Jelly Roll's compositions were greatly influenced by Joplin's. Louis Armstrong credited Joplin as the principal source of Jelly Roll's ideas, and Lottie Joplin would later state, "In the early 1900's Jelly and another man named Porter King were working on a number of their own. Apparently, they got stuck. Anyway, they mailed it off to Scott, asking him to help. Later, when he completed it, Scott mailed it back, but it didn't get published until years afterward. By then, Scott and Porter King were dead, so Jelly named it after his old friend, calling it 'King Porter Stomp.'"[9]

Scott Joplin's compositions had provided his ticket out of the sporting district. Teaching was far more suited to his temperament than holding his own in boisterous, smoke-filled saloons against young upstarts who could not write a note. Though he would perform on occasion, Scott Joplin's commitment to the composing tradition was firm, and his works from then on would indicate his feelings about the proper course for ragtime—elevation to a serious musical form, not denigration to a carnival sound.

Perhaps with this in mind, and encouraged by Ernst, Scott returned to work on *The Ragtime Dance*, hoping that Stark would agree to publish it. The work was a source of continued dissent between the author and his publisher, and may be the reason why Joplin himself published his next work. "The Easy Winners," issued in October 1901, bears on its cover the logo "Published by Scott Joplin, St. Louis, Mo." and carried also the legend "Composed by Scott Joplin: King of Ragtime Writers." As it is a fine piece, melodic and flowing, Scott Joplin was probably not *forced* to publish it himself. It has been suggested that Stark, being puritanical in nature, might have been loath to publish a piece that glorified sport, including horse racing (four different sports are depicted on the cover).[10] However, if this were so, Joplin could easily have sold the composition to another publisher. It is probable that Joplin chose to publish the piece himself to demonstrate independence, a subtle warning to Stark that Joplin was dependent on no one publisher.

Publication of "The Easy Winners" in October 1901 may also have been planned as a method of persuasion to get Stark to reconsider his refusal to publish *The Rag-time Dance*, for toward the end of 1901 Joplin presented his performance again, this time in a private hall and for the Stark family alone. Among those present was John Stark's daughter Nell, who had recently returned from studying music in Europe. Impressed by the performance, she prevailed upon her father to publish it.[11] Pressured from several directions, Stark nevertheless remained firm in his opposition, and the rift between the two men widened.

So Joplin bypassed Stark in publishing two more compositions. In April, 1902, "I Am Thinking of My Picka-ninny Days," his first song since "A Picture of Her Face" (issued in 1895), was published by Thiebes-Stierlin Music Company of St. Louis. Written with his friend Henry Jackson, who composed the lyrics, the song was in the still popular romantic and sentimental Stephen Foster vein, and beautifully harmonized so as to appeal to a bar-bershop quartet type of rendition. Joplin may well have written it primarily for the money, although it reportedly did not sell very well. In May, S. Simon of St. Louis issued "Cleopha," a "March and Two-Step" that enjoyed immediate popularity and became a favorite piece for the John Philip Sousa band.

Scott Joplin may have been quiet, rarely speaking in a voice higher than a whisper. He may have been sensitive to the sort of criticism he had borne from the "cutters." But no one had ever called him wishy-washy. As a young-ster he had been determined to make something of him-self. As an adult, he was equally determined. For him, it was not enough to be published. He wanted to compose and publish an elevated type of music. And, as John Stark was learning, he could be downright ornery about it. In the meantime, Stark was probably experiencing some guilt feelings as well as concern about finances. He was aware of the importance of "Maple Leaf Rag" to the success of his business, the acquisition of a fine house for his family at 3967 Cleveland Avenue, and an excellent business plant at 306 N. Eighteenth Street. At length he consented to publish *The Ragtime Dance.*

With Stark's promise secured, Joplin returned to the John Stark & Son fold, and toward the end of 1902, Stark issued two Joplin pieces, "March Majestic" and "The Strenuous Life." The first is a fine work that marks Joplin's coming to maturity as a composer of marches; the second is a not particularly distinguished rag. But these were hardly all of Joplin's publications with Stark that year. Partly because his life style was now much more conducive to composing, partly because Stark had agreed to publish his dance composition, and partly, perhaps, to show his detractors that performance was not all there was to ragtime, Scott Joplin was extremely prolific that year. At the end of 1902, three more of his works were published, almost simultaneously with *The Ragtime Dance,* bringing the number of his works published in that single year to eight.

The three works were "A Breeze from Alabama," "Elite Syncopations," and "The Entertainer." Of the three, the first is weakest, another march two-step, dedicated to "P. G. Lowery, World's Challenging Colored Cornetist and Band Master." "Elite Syncopations" is, as its title suggests, only modestly syncopated and meant to be played in the steady Joplin tempo. "Not fast," the note over the first bar cautions, and such instructions appear over and over again in published Joplin compositions. Interestingly, they begin with the first Stark publications in St. Louis and indicate Joplin's reaction to the new, faster style of playing he encountered in that city. From then on, in whatever terms he couched his instructions—"moderato," "slow," "not fast," "not too fast"—Joplin exercised his composer's prerogative over the mere performer.

"The Entertainer" carries these instructions ("not fast"). Some of its melodies recall the plucking of mandolins, instruments that were popular in that day, played by small groups of wandering string musicians called "serenaders"; and the rag is dedicated to "James Brown and his Mandolin Club." Melodious, with a happy and restful quality about it, in terms of sales, the piece was the most successful of Joplin's 1902 publications[12] and it is the best known of Joplin's works today as a result of Joshua Rifkin's recording and its adaptation by Marvin Hamlisch in the score of the motion picture *The Sting*. Its title may have come from the Sedalia period, when the Maple Leaf Club advertised Scott Joplin as "the Entertainer." However it is unlikely that Joplin had any say in the choice of the sheet music cover, which depicts a black in caricature, his feet fully as long as the area between his knees and his ankles—a "coon" type cover of the sort that Stark generally avoided. Not that Joplin had a mid-twentieth-century type of black consciousness: some of the words in the opening section of his piece *The Ragtime Dance* are embarrassing by today's standards—references to "coon," "razor fight," and "dark town," for example.

The lyrics notwithstanding, *The Ragtime Dance* was Joplin's answer to the prevailing association of ragtime with lowlife. Essentially a folk ballet, it is not a denial of folkways but a presentation of them in a sympathetic, joyful light. Some of Joplin's finest musical passages are con-

tained in this piece, whose words give little indication of
either the melody or the choreography:

> Let me see you do the "rag time dance,"
> Turn left and do the "cake walk prance,"
> Turn the other way and do the "slow drag"—
>
> Now take your lady to the World's Fair
> And do the "rag time dance."
>
> Let me see you do the "clean up dance,"
> Now you do the "Jennie Cooler dance,"
> Turn the other way and do the "slow drag"—
>
> Now take your lady to the World's Fair
> And do the "rag time dance."[13]

The entire piece filled nine printed pages and was very
expensive to produce. Stark issued it reluctantly, still convinced that it would not sell well. It required more than
twenty minutes to perform and was beyond the ability of
the average parlor pianist. But Joplin was pleased, productive once more, and for that Stark could be thankful.

For his part, Joplin was optimistic about sales and already well into his first ragtime opera, which he had
titled *A Guest of Honor,* news of which probably caused
John Stark to groan privately. Actually, an opera by a
black man was not unheard of. Harry Lawrence Freeman,
a Negro, had written *The Martyr* some years before, and
it had been produced in Denver in 1893.[14] *A Guest of
Honor* was one act in length and contained twelve tunes,
all rags. Joplin was certain it would be popular; John
Stark was not so sure.

Besides publishing more works that year than in any
previous or subsequent single year, Joplin was beginning

to receive more than merely local newspaper publicity. W. H. Carter, editor of the Sedalia *Times*, visited St. Louis in April. Some years before, he had written editorials criticizing as mere "piano-thumping" the music pouring out of the smoke-filled rooms of Main Street. By 1902, however, he had been swept up in the ragtime tide and, on his return to Sedalia from St. Louis, praised Joplin in one of his articles:

> . . . Mr. Scott Joplin, who is gaining a world's reputation as the Rag Time King. Mr. Joplin is only writing, composing and collecting his money from the different music houses in St. Louis, Chicago, New York and a number of other cities. Among his numbers that are largely in demand in the above cities are the "Maple Leaf Club" [*sic*], "Easy Winners," "Rag Time Dance" and "Peacherine," all of which are used by the leading players and orchestras.[15]

The St. Louis Fair was scheduled to open in 1903, and Tom Turpin wrote a rag in honor of the event, "St. Louis Rag." While it was an excellent piece, unfortunately it turned out to be premature, for the opening of the fair was postponed until 1904, destroying the initial sales potential of the composition. Various people and situations were blamed for the delay, none of which caused Tom Turpin to feel any better. However, he had other reasons to be happy that year, for it was the year in which he opened what would become the most famous of the various Turpin establishments, the Rosebud Bar.[16]

Located at 2220–22 Market Street, and reportedly a multifaceted business that included gambling and prostitution upstairs, it was open "all night and day" and immediately became a favorite hangout for the best ragtime performers and for the youngsters who sought to learn from the masters. Indeed, it was advertised as a "Head-quarters for Colored Professionals." There was no question how important the piano was to Turpin. He had it on blocks about a foot high so one had to stand up to reach its keys. "He wouldn't let just anybody play it either," Charlie Thompson once recalled.[17] Scott Joplin was among the few who were allowed access to it, and in fact he was invited to play whenever he dropped by. In that friendly atmosphere, Joplin would indeed perform on occasion—always his own compositions and always exactly as they were written—but no one showed any disrespect, not in Tom Turpin's place.

The Rosebud was not to be merely a saloon. Turpin quickly took steps to establish it among higher classes of society as well, and in 1902 he would inaugurate the first of many annual Rosebud Balls held in a large hall and featuring a piano contest. All the "best people in town" would attend.

In 1903, the Joplins and the Haydens moved to 2117 Lucas Avenue, where Will Joplin lived. They rented a number of rooms, some of which Belle in turn rented to visiting musicians who sought out Joplin.[18] It was a happy period for Scott. His compositions were selling respectably well, and new ideas came to him easily. Work on *A Guest of Honor* was progressing and he was optimistic about the future.

In February, Scott wrote to the Copyright Office in Washington, D.C., to apply for a copyright for the opera,[19] probably indicating in his letter that the manuscript copies were on their way under separate cover. Shortly thereafter he began rehearsing his drama com-

pany for a performance. The April 1903 issue of the
Sedalia *Times* printed the following item:

> Scott Hayden has been in the city all week visiting parents
> and friends. He has signed a contract with the Scott Joplin
> Drama Company of St. Louis in which Latisha Howell and
> Arthur Marshall are performers.

Arthur Marshall had arrived in St. Louis in 1902–3
after two years playing piano on tour with McCabe's
Minstrels. According to Marshall,[20] the opera was presented in a large dance hall in St. Louis and was quite
well received—well enough to attract two of the major
booking agencies in the city, Majestic and Haviland, who
were interested in producing it. Joplin, of course, was also
interested in the opera's publication, and the Stark family
had been invited to the performance. The Starks were
fairly pleased with the opera, but according to legend
felt that Joplin should write a stronger libretto. Joplin
thought his book was strong enough as written.

Meanwhile, the school of ragtime known as Tin Pan
Alley had arisen in New York City, primarily because
New York was the center of the music publishing business
but also because it was a large and busy city, demanding
tempos speedier and more "nervous" than did other
places. It was a commercialized style of ragtime, the style
with which we in the latter twentieth century are most
familiar. Also, it was primarily a ragtime played by white
men, of whom composer Ben Harney was perhaps the
earliest and most famous example. It was another example of whites adopting and exploiting an initially black
form. These considerations must be borne in mind when

reading the following, written by a prominent Tin Pan Alley composer, Monroe H. Rosenfeld, and which appeared in the June 7, 1903, issue of the St. Louis *Globe-Democrat:*

St. Louis boasts of a composer of music, who despite the ebony hue of his features and a retiring disposition, has written possibly more instrumental successes than any other local composer. His name is Scott Joplin, and he is better known as "The King of Rag Time Writers" because of the many famous works in syncopated melodies which he has written. He has, however, also penned other classes of music and various local numbers of note.

Scott Joplin was reared and educated in St. Louis. His first notable success in instrumental music was the "Maple Leaf Rag" of which thousands and thousands of copies have been sold. A year or two ago Mr. John Stark, a publisher of this city and father of Miss Eleanor Stark, the well known piano virtuoso, bought the manuscript of "Maple Leaf" from Joplin. Almost within a month from the date of its issue this quaint creation became a byword with musicians and within another half a twelfth-month, circulated itself throughout the nation in vast numbers. This composition was speedily followed by others of a like character. Until now the Stark list embraces nearly a score of the Joplin effusions . . .

Probably the best and most euphonious of his latter day compositions is "The Entertainer." It is a jingling work of a very original character, embracing various strains of a retentive character which set the foot in spontaneous action and leave an indelible imprint on the tympanum . . .

Rosenfeld's factual errors regarding Joplin's birthplace, the year "Maple Leaf Rag" was published and the early success of the piece notwithstanding,[21] this is a remarkable tribute to a black composer of classical ragtime from a white composer of "pop" ragtime. Men like Rosenfeld were publishing rags that sold far better than most of Joplin's; in addition, they were schooled in a radically different style of performance. And yet, a discerning man like Rosenfeld could see Joplin's brilliance and praise it publicly. The Rosenfeld article continues:

> Joplin's ambition is to shine in other spheres. He affirms that it is only a pastime for him to compose syncopated music and he longs for more arduous work. To this end he is assiduously toiling upon an opera, nearly a score of the numbers of which he has already composed and which he hopes to give an early production [in] this city.

It is clear that Joplin sorely wanted to establish a reputation as a composer of operas and ballets, of serious works—not the simple rags he effortlessly dashed off. But as 1903 wore on, it appeared that such a reputation would not be established through the sales of his works. *The Ragtime Dance* was selling poorly, as John Stark had expected it would. The two still had not come to an agreement on *A Guest of Honor*. Once again a rift developed between the idealistic composer and the business-minded publisher.

Again Scott Joplin decided to show John Stark that he didn't need the company as much as the company needed him. All four of the Joplin pieces published in 1903 were issued by other publishers. The Val A. Reis Music Company of St. Louis brought out "Weeping Willow" and a second Joplin-Hayden collaboration, "Something Doing."

Victor Kremer of Chicago published "Palm Leaf Rag," and Success Music Company, also of Chicago, issued a song, "Little Black Baby."[22]

The first three works are unmistakably in the Joplin tradition, and all are very songlike, perhaps indicating his concentration on his opera at the time. Both "Weeping Willow" and "Palm Leaf Rag" have about them a "plantation melody" aura that is especially evident in "Weeping Willow," which Trebor Jay Tichenor, for one, considers one of his most moving creations. Deceptively light in format, it has about it a dark and introspective air. Thus, the title is very descriptive.[23] "Something Doing," the second collaboration between Joplin and Hayden, has given rise to controversy over which composer contributed what elements. It is a smoothly flowing, rhythmic, and melodious piece, clearly a whole, not a collection of parts. Although no mention is made of Joplin's earlier works on the cover, the cover illustration contains elements clearly borrowed from the first cover of "Maple Leaf Rag." A Negro couple, dressed in their finery and on their way to a cakewalk, are depicted in almost the same position, but reversed as in a mirror image, as one of the couples on the "Maple Leaf Rag" cover, and the decorations on the man's sleeve and on the hook of his cane are similar. The "Something Doing" cover, however, depicts a gallery of well-to-do white people ogling (some using opera glasses) the couple and acting thoroughly amused. A "coon cover" of the more genteel sort, to be sure, but a "coon cover" nevertheless.

"Little Black Baby" is best forgotten. Clearly a potboiler, it may have been done by Joplin as a favor to Louise Armstrong Bristol, who wrote the words and copyrighted it. Joplin's name does not even appear on the cover, an omission he may have insisted on. The publisher, Success Music Company, was a vanity press, and indeed no other publisher but a vanity press would likely have accepted it. A sample of the lyrics: "What says dis little black baby to little black mammy by its side? Goo-goo-goo-e, goo-garee-goo; Tra-la-la-ra-ba-ma-oo." Somewhat puzzling is that the cover illustration is of a *white* baby. Joplin's melody is fittingly trite.

It is interesting to speculate that Joplin may have collaborated on the song to earn some extra money for the care of his own baby, for probably sometime in early 1903 a baby daughter was born to Scott Joplin and Belle Hayden.[24]

Both parents greeted the event with hope that the child would bring them closer together. They had not been getting along very well. To get along with Scott Joplin, a woman either had to share his consuming interest in music or understand him enough to nurture him in his interest and not to resent it. Belle apparently did neither. Scott spent long hours shut up in his study, composing at his oak rolltop desk and at his beloved piano, leaving her alone for extended periods of time; and perhaps when he did have time to give her the attention she sorely required she complained to him and forced him away. Not to put the blame entirely on Belle, Joplin appears to have been very critical of her lack of musical talent, although he must have been aware of it from the start. He may have been a very demanding genius. If the birth of their daughter was a source of hope for an improved relationship, that hope was soon dashed. Ill from birth, the little girl lived only a few months, and with her death all hope for the Joplins' relationship seems to have died too. Arthur Marshall's stated recollection of the situation is a sensitive and tactful one:

> Mrs. Joplin wasn't so interested in music and her taking violin lessons from Scott was a perfect failure. Mr. Joplin was seriously humiliated. Of course unpleasant attitudes and lack of home interests occurred between them.
>
> They finally separated. He told me his wife had no interest in his music career. Otherwise Mrs. Joplin was very pleasant to his friends and especially to we home boys. But the other side was strictly theirs. To other acquaintances of the family other than I and Hayden and also my brother Lee who knew the facts, Scott was towards her in their presence very pleasing. A shield of honor toward her existed and for the child. As my brother . . . Hayden and I were like his brothers, Joplin often asked us to console Mrs. Joplin—perhaps she would reconsider. But she remained neutral. She never was harsh with us, but we just couldn't get her to see the point. So a separation finally resulted.[25]

Probably the Joplins parted in the late summer or early fall of 1903. He moved out of the house on Lucas Avenue and to a room in the house where the Turpins lived, but he would not stay there long. The past few months had been fraught with tension and unhappiness. St. Louis held unpleasant memories for him, and before long he would leave the city.

CHAPTER VI

On the Move Again

In the fall of 1903, Scott took his drama company, re-named the Scott Joplin Ragtime Opera Company, on tour with *A Guest of Honor*. His first extended period of traveling in some years, the tour took him to Iowa and possibly to Nebraska, as well as to other parts of Missouri.[1] At first, Joplin enjoyed being on the road again. He was greeted as a celebrity in red-light districts and honky-tonks wherever he went, and in the cities and towns far away from St. Louis once again he felt free to go to the taverns and saloons and play his compositions without feeling self-conscious. But within a month the tour was beset by difficulties. There was dissension among the twelve members of the company and by the time they had played their way through Missouri and reached Iowa, the troupe was in serious trouble.

Were there disagreements between Joplin and the members of his company over *A Guest of Honor* or was the dissension merely a result of conflicting personalities? We will probably never know. We do know that the opera company disbanded and at least five members took leave of the rest. With the remaining members Joplin quickly formed a minstrel show, the cast probably pooling their talents and material remembered from other shows in which they had performed. However, this make-shift minstrel show was not successful either. Items in the "Correspondence" section of the New York *Dramatic Mirror* in September and October 1903 graphically tell the story:

September 12, 1903
  Missouri, Webb City—New Blake Theatre: Scott Joplin Ragtime Opera Co. 12

October 17, 1903
  Iowa, Ottumwa—Grand Opera House: Joplin Opera Co. Sept. 29 failed to appear; reported disbanded
  Mason City—Parker's Opera House: Scott Joplin Opera Co. 12
  Nebraska, Fremont—New Larson: Joplin Ragtime Minstrels 7
  Beatrice—Paddock Opera House: Scott Joplin's Ragtime Minstrels 6

October 24, 1903
  Iowa, Mason City—Wilson Theatre: Scott Joplin Opera Co. 12 canceled
  Nebraska, Fremont—Love's Theatre: Joplin Minstrels 7 canceled.

The failure of the tour must have been a heavy blow for Joplin, but if he had any apprehensions about returning to St. Louis, they were dispelled when he arrived back in the city. Perhaps having heard of the abortive tour and wishing to show their support, the people of the district welcomed him with a parade along Market Street.

Thereafter, every time he returned to St. Louis he was greeted with such a parade.[2]

In late 1903 or early 1904, Joplin returned to Sedalia, taking a room at 124 West Cooper and listing himself in the 1904 city directory under "music." He had known happy times in Sedalia and perhaps he felt the need to return there for that reason. He would visit St. Louis from time to time, but he did not return for Tom Turpin's third annual Rosebud Ball and piano-playing contest. The absence of his name is noticeable in the following account of the event that appeared in the February 27, 1904, issue of the St. Louis *Palladium:*

> On Tuesday last the Rose Bud club gave its third annual ball and piano contest at the New Douglass hall . . . and it was one of the largest, finest and best-conducted affairs of the kind ever held in St. Louis. The hall was packed and jammed, many being unable to gain admission, and the crowd was composed, well-dressed, good-looking and orderly people, from all classes of society. A great many of the best people in town were present, among them being The Palladium man, to enjoy the festivities and witness the great piano contest.
>
> Mr. Tom Turpin presented an elegant gold medal to the successful contestant, Mr. Louis Chauvin. Messrs. Joe Jordan and Charles Warfield were a tie for second place . . . The club desires to thank their many friends for their generous support, and promises on the occasion of their next annual ball to see to it that every piano player of note in the United States enters, and will give an elegant diamond medal to the winner . . . Mr. Samuel Patterson came from Chicago just to attend the Turpin ball.[3]

By the time Scott returned to St. Louis, John Stark was looking more favorably on *A Guest of Honor*. Whether this change of heart involved his desire not to lose Joplin's friendship or business is not known; certainly it was not because of the abortive tour. Plans to publish the work went ahead, and despite the fact that their initial five-year contract was up, Joplin would publish two excellent rags with John Stark & Son. Two other pieces published that year were issued by other firms. One was "The Favorite," the rag that was sold to A. W. Perry & Sons back in 1899 and whose publication Joplin may have requested delayed until his contract with Stark was completed.[4] The other was "The Sycamore," published by Will Rossiter in Chicago, where Joplin probably visited while on tour with his opera company. Billed as "A Concert Rag," it indicates Joplin's increasingly ambitious attitude toward ragtime and has been described by some as a "ragtime etude."

The St. Louis Fair finally opened on April 30, 1904. Huge, lavish, it was eagerly greeted by the district, for the out-of-towners would bring many dollars to spend there when they came to the fair. Come they did. From its opening at the end of April to the closing on December 1, an average of more than 100,000 new visitors came each day, and of course many visited again and again. It was a fascinating exhibition, including the largest number of foreign exhibits of any fair to date. Electric lights were everywhere—an exciting new invention—and one hundred automobiles were on display, one of which had actually made the trip from New York to St. Louis "on its own power."[5]

One of the major attractions of the fair was the Cascades Gardens, a huge watercourse of falls and fountains, ponds and lagoons that flowed down the main thoroughfare. Capitalizing on and memorializing the fair's main attraction, Joplin wrote "The Cascades" and caught in it the bubble and flow of the watercourse. It was billed as "The Masterpiece of Scott Joplin," an accolade that Joplin probably liked. Evidently, he also liked the photograph of himself that appeared in an oval frame on the cover of the first edition of the sheet music, for he used the same photograph on a rag published by another company five years later.

One of Stark's advertisements for "The Cascades" poked fun at those who deplored ragtime without understanding it:

A FIERCE TRAGEDY IN ONE ACT

SCENE: A Fashionable Theatre. Enter Mrs. Van Clausenberg and party—late, of course.

MRS. VAN C: "What is the orchestra playing? It is the grandest thing I have ever heard. It is positively inspiring."
YOUNG AMERICA (*in the seat behind*): "Why that is the 'Cascades' by Joplin."
MRS. VAN C: "Well, that is one on me. I thought I had heard all of the great music, but this is the most thrilling piece I have ever heard. I suppose Joplin is a Pole who was educated in Paris."
YOUNG AM.: "Not so you could notice it. He's a young Negro from Texarkana, and the piece they are playing is a rag."

Sensation—Perturbation—Trepidation—and Seven Other Kinds of Emotion.

MRS. VAN C.: "****** The idea. The very word ragtime rasps my finer sensibilities. (*Rising*) I'm going home and I'll never come to this theatre again. I just can't stand trashy music."[6]

Stark is understandably laudatory, but he is not alone. In the opinion of many musicologists, "The Cascades" is one of the peaks of classic ragtime, one of the best of Joplin's works. Its happy, swinging elements show Joplin's rare ability to adapt the folk rhythms and moods that are the source of ragtime in a continually creative and refined manner. Most other rag composers at this time had stalled in a rote formula and were simply "ragging" already established forms. Joplin was constantly developing the possibilities of ragtime and improving his compositional abilities through study, on his own and with Ernst. Among his personal effects when he died was a well-thumbed and marginally notated copy of *A Manual of Simple, Double, Triple, and Quadruple Counterpoint.*[7]

"The Chrysanthemum," the other work published by Stark in 1904, shows Joplin's continued search, aided by Alfred Ernst, into the classical possibilities of rag. Subtitled "An Afro-Intermezzo," it has no discernible African elements in it other than those out of which the bases of ragtime developed. Marked "Fine" with a firm, final chord, it represents a further exploration into classical form and has a minimum of syncopation. Like many of Joplin's works, however, it has a deep, introspective quality. Indeed, Stark advertised that Joplin wrote the composition as a result of a dream he had after reading *Alice's Adventures in Wonderland,* and the fantasy-aura about it lends credence to this legend.[8]

Sometime in late 1904–early 1905, Stark moved his family to 4500 Shenandoah Street in St. Louis and established his business in the city. He is listed in the 1905 City Directory as President, Music Printing and Publishing Company. Largely due to Scott Joplin, Stark was becoming highly successful. For his part, Joplin may have felt that Stark owed him more serious consideration of *A Guest of Honor* for publication, given his relative loyalty to the publisher. It appears that they were disagreeing again, for Stark published only one of the Joplin works issued in 1905. Called "Rosebud Two-Step," and dedicated to "my friend Tom Turpin," it is a gay march in the typical two-step pattern and destined for some fame not so much because of its tune as because of its name.

Of the six works Joplin published that year, four are named for women. Only once before, in 1902, had he published a composition with a woman's name—"Cleopha." And only one more would be so named after "Antoinette," published in 1906. "Bethena" is a waltz, and one of the finest Joplin ever published. Subtitled "A Concert Waltz," it is perhaps the first true ragtime waltz ever written. An enchanting, almost haunting melody, its mood is heightened by the photograph of a beautiful black girl on the cover. Who was Bethena? Perhaps she was just a beautiful girl whose photograph was chosen by the T. Bahnsen Piano Manufacturing Company, which published the work. The same company published the other Joplin waltz to be issued that year, "Binks' Waltz," which has little in the way of comparison with "Bethena." A pleasant waltz in the polite Victorian style, it seems to have been written for children, with which its cover is illustrated. The same company published the Joplin song of that year, "Sarah Dear," with words written by Joplin's friend and member of the Scott Joplin Drama Company, Henry Jackson. It is not an entirely original tune. The chorus is the same tune used in the Ben Harny rag "St. Louis Tickle." But the tune wasn't original to Harney either, for it had long been in use as a riverboat drinking song.

Will Rossiter, a Chicago firm that had published Joplin before, issued "Eugenia" that year. The first page of the composition contains the blurb: "Notice! Don't play this piece fast, It is never right to play 'Ragtime' fast. Author." Clearly, Joplin was becoming increasingly concerned with what he considered the adulteration of ragtime by those who emphasized speed over form. Clearly also, he was not yet comfortable with the term *ragtime*, setting it off by quotation marks as if he still considered it a colloquialism. "Eugenia" is an involved piece of writing, done specifically, as the cover says, "for Band and Orchestra." Some musicologists hail it as the first of the mature Joplin pieces; others bemoan its lack of spontaneity.[9]

The final piece bearing a woman's name is "Leola," issued by a new publisher for Joplin, American Music Syndicate of St. Louis. This, too, carries the warning not to play it fast. Like "Eugenia," is seems to indicate a Joplin striving for form over spontaneity, but it is not as successful as "Eugenia." Although it is the first Joplin piece to have been copyrighted simultaneously in Britain,[10] it did not sell particularly well and indeed did not come to light until the 1950s. What makes it an interesting document is its possible biographical importance, for despite its dedication to "Miss Minnie Wade," the composition is likely named for a woman with whom Joplin was in love. Ragtimer Charlie Thompson once said "Joplin's one love was a girl named Leola who jilted him! For sometime afterward he was not interested in women."[11] Were Bethena and Eugenia, and, later, Antoinette real women too? We may never know.

It would seem that Scott Joplin was rather unlucky with women in that period of his life. By contrast, he attracted young musicians who, having met him, and even before actually making his acquaintance, idolized him and were forever loyal to him. In that year a nineteen-year-old named James Scott came briefly into his life. Scott had been born in Neosho, Missouri, in 1886, and had moved with his parents first to Ottawa, Kansas, and then to Carthage, Missouri, where his father purchased his first piano for him. When he was sixteen, he went to work for Dumars music store, washing windows. When the owner learned that he could read and play music, James was put to work plugging the latest tunes. He had a natural talent for composition, and his first work, "A Summer Breeze—March and Two Step," was published by Dumars in early 1903, when he was just seventeen years old. By 1904 two more compositions sold respectably in the area, but not enough to constitute a going business. Dumars ceased publishing, and Scott set off for St. Louis to find a new publishing company.

One of his favorite pieces, and one that had often inspired him, was "Maple Leaf Rag." Finding himself in St. Louis, and learning that Scott Joplin was in town for a visit, he located the master and asked him to listen to his work. Flattered by the youth's attention and always interested in young talent, Joplin listened to Scott's rag and, recognizing merit in it, introduced the youth to John Stark and recommended that Stark purchase the work. Stark published it the next year as "Frog Legs Rag." Joplin had little way of knowing that the young man he had helped would later become one of the only two composers considered on the same level as he was—indeed, second only to him.[12]

For his own part, Scott Joplin seems to have entered a very nonproductive period toward the end of 1905. Perhaps his having been jilted by Leola affected him; perhaps he was simply "written out" after having produced a number of fine pieces. Whatever the reason, he apparently decided it was time to hit the road again, and sometime late in 1905 he set out for Chicago, where Arthur Marshall was living with his bride and playing at Lewis's Saloon[13] and where Louis Chauvin had become firmly and fatally ensconced in that city's red-light district.

Scott stayed with Marshall while he rather half-heartedly made the rounds of the music publishers.[14] It is likely that he did not have a substantial amount of material to offer, and he seems to have been primarily interested in making contacts, in case he decided to remain in Chicago. Making his way to the city's red-light district, he met with Louis Chauvin, an experience that was not likely to have increased his optimism about the lot of a black ragtime composer. The brilliant young composer-pianist who had won the piano contest at Tom Turpin's Rosebud Ball back in February 1904 was only twenty-two, but it was tragically evident that he would not live to be thirty. Like too many other young members of the musical subculture, he had become addicted to drugs and had contracted syphilis. He and Sam Patterson were still together, the more stable Patterson concerned about his friend but powerless to help him.

Chauvin smoked opium constantly and was already showing signs of the terminal syphilis that would eventually kill him in 1908, but he continued to compose, creating the most exquisite themes at times. Unfortunately, he remained too undisciplined to incorporate these themes into a finished, and publishable, work.

Thanks to Scott Joplin, at least some of those themes were eventually published in "Heliotrope Bouquet—A Slow Drag Two-Step." When Joplin visited Chauvin in a bawdyhouse parlor, he was shocked at the young man's appearance and physical condition, but he had seen such things before and knew there was little he could do. He inquired about Chauvin's composing and was promptly treated to a rendition of two beautiful themes. Perhaps aware that the best thing he could do for his young friend was to get those themes published, he promptly sat down at the parlor piano and composed two themes of his own. Sam Patterson, who witnessed the event, marveled at Joplin's ability to work out two complementary themes on the spur of the moment.[15] Joplin and Chauvin worked together a while longer, smoothing over the rough places, but it was Joplin who did the final polishing, Chauvin's mood being too fitful to permit extended concentration on any one thing even if it was to be one of the few published works to bear his name.

During his stay in Chicago, Joplin also worked on a collaborative piece with Arthur Marshall. In this piece, too, the work of Joplin's collaborator came first, in the two beginning strains, while the trio and final strain were Joplin's. It attested to Joplin's genius and to his generosity that he allowed his protégés to set the tone of the piece in his collaborations with them, and composed material that complemented theirs. The Joplin-Marshall collaboration, "Lily Queen—A Ragtime Two-Step," would be published in 1907, the same year that "Heliotrope Bouquet—A Slow Drag Two-Step" would be issued.

After staying with Marshall for a few weeks, Scott found a place of his own at 2840 Armour Avenue and listed himself as a musician in the 1906 city directory. But he did not stay in Chicago long. According to Arthur Marshall, he was very eager to go to New York.[16] John Stark had just moved there, establishing his publishing business at 127 East Twenty-third Street. New York was undeniably the center of the music publishing business in the United States, and Scott, now that he had no real ties in the Midwest, was eager to try his own luck there. He did not go immediately to New York, however. Psychologically, he was not prepared for such a major move. While maintaining contact with Stark, he returned to St. Louis, using the Turpin place as a base while he toured the area vaudeville circuit.[17]

Too disturbed mentally to compose very much, and too unsettled to make a living teaching music, he succumbed to performing again. At times, he enjoyed it, especially going out to Clayton, Missouri, with newspaperman Harry La Mertha, with whom he collaborated on a pot-boiler song called "Snoring Sampson."

It was a time of rather aimless wandering for Scott, and perhaps in an attempt to re-establish his equilibrium he returned to his roots. Sometime in 1907 he went back to Texarkana, the first time he had been home in several years.[18]

Sadly, his mother was not alive to see him. Florence Joplin had died some years earlier, in her early sixties.[19] A strong, determined woman, Florence had managed to support herself to the end. A few years after Scott had left Texarkana, Canaan Baptist Church had moved from the old Hide house into its own building on Laurel between Eighth and Ninth Streets.[20] Florence had become caretaker of that church, performing a variety of functions. She scrubbed the floors and kept the lamps filled with oil. "She was a little bitty woman, couldn't have weighed more than ninety pounds," recalls George Mosley. "I'd often go down and get the lamps off the wall for her and put oil in them so she wouldn't have to do it." Florence also rang the church bell, which was employed to announce church services or otherwise to call the congregation together, and to report deaths in the community. "That old lady rang the bell whenever somebody died," says Mosley. "If it was midnight and she got the word, she tolled that bell. And she had a way of tolling it that would tell you whether it was a child or an old person, or a middle-aged person. The way she tolled that bell . . ."[21]

Florence had lived to see all her children grow up. Monroe, who had gone to live with his father and Laura before Scott left to go on the road, had married and had two children, Mattie and Fred, by his first wife, who had subsequently died. Later, around 1900–1, he had married his second wife, Rosa, by whom he'd had two more children, Donita and Ethel. Robert had married a woman named Cora and had a daughter, Essie,[22] but the marriage had failed, and around 1901 he had left Texarkana to join his brothers Scott and Will in St. Louis. Both Osie and Myrtle had worked as cooks and sung in and around the area before marrying and moving into Arkansas.[23] While only Scott had achieved any renown, none of Florence's children had died or been imprisoned, and all had learned trades of some sort, in itself a source of pride for a black mother in Texas at the turn of the century.

Scott's father, Jiles, was still very much alive, although he no longer worked for the railroad. Swinging the huge mauls to pound spikes into the tracks, dragging the heavy sections of track, and heaving them into place had been tough, backbreaking work. Indeed, the average working life of a railroad laborer was between ten and fifteen years. Jiles had developed leg trouble, and though he had still listed himself in the 1906 Texarkana City Directory as a laborer, he had done little heavy labor for some years. Now, at the age of sixty-four, he hobbled around on a stick and did yard work when he felt up to it.[24]

Some years earlier, he and Laura had separated.[25] Zenobia Campbell recalled, "The boarding house lady [at 830 Laurel Street] tried to get him and his second wife back together, but it didn't do any good. They never did live together anymore."[26] When Scott returned to Texarkana in 1907, Jiles was living with Monroe and Rosa at 815 Ash Street, and during his visit Scott, too, stayed with his older brother and family.

Scott's visit was one of the most exciting events the family could remember. Not only was he a famous composer of music, but he was a brother and son who had traveled, who had been to the big cities of St. Louis and Chicago, met famous and interesting people, and, not least, seen his two brothers, Robert and Will, neither of whom had evidently been home in some years. "They kept him up all day till late at night," recalls Scott's nephew, Fred.[27]

Scott's return was also a major event in the life of the Texarkana black community, and an occurrence of some interest to the white community as well, for Scott was a "home boy" who had made good, the composer of piano pieces that were played on parlor pianos and performed by itinerant pianists across the country. Scott was aware of his position as a returning hero and exploited it for what he could. As George Mosley puts it, "Well, he did act kind of famous." Soon after Scott's arrival, he went down to the Beasley Music Store and began to play some of his compositions on the piano in the back room of the store, attracting passers-by, and word quickly spread that not only was Scott Joplin back in town, but also he was playing his famous music. They gathered around him and questioned him about his life, openly admiring. "When they came home, it was after midnight," Fred Joplin recalls. It was an exhilarating experience for Scott, and though it was late, he sat right down at the Joplins' parlor piano and continued playing. "He was playing," says Fred Joplin, "I heard the music and I got out of bed and just sat there, listening."[28]

Fred Joplin remembers something else, although his memory is hazy. During an interview in 1976 he said that by the time Scott returned to Texarkana around 1907 he had been to Germany. "He was playing somewhere and a German got in with him and when he [the German] went back to Germany he carried Scott back with him. . . . So he went over there, and I don't know how long he stayed. But when he did come back, he had played so much and wrote a lot of music and he had started his fame." Although none of the other Texarkanans interviewed could recall any mention of a German or a trip to Germany by Scott, these statements of Fred Joplin's are intriguing. The possibility that Scott did visit Europe continues to be a viable one, and hopefully someday someone will be able to document it.

The days were filled with music. Mattie, Monroe's eldest daughter, was studying music, and Scott taught her to play "Maple Leaf Rag" on the parlor piano.[29] And he played at least once at one of the weekly dances held at J. C. Johnson's pavilion down on Ninth Street.[30] Perhaps one of the most gratifying aspects of Scott's visit was being able to show his old teacher and mentor that he had made good. Johnson was a classicist and it is likely that he did not entirely approve of Scott's ragtime compositions, but he would have understood and encouraged his former pupil's urge to create ragtime opera. Perhaps Scott played excerpts from *The Ragtime Dance* and *A Guest of Honor* for Johnson.

Scott stayed only a few days in Texarkana before he was off again, to return no more. He left behind him warm feelings and happy memories, and the seed of a small amount of family dissension, for his uncle's visit had caused Fred Joplin to decide he wanted to be a piano player too. "I wanted to play like my uncle. That's what started me wanting to play, was seeing him. So I started banging on the piano, and in six years I had learned it so good that I played for all the commencement exercises. But my aunties, who were school teachers, they wanted me to be a doctor. 'We don't want no piano player,' they said."[31] Fred says that the family did not talk about Scott much after he left; perhaps they did not want to encourage Fred.

Scott returned to the Midwest and eventually settled for a time in St. Louis. His spirits lifted somewhat after his visit with his family, but his productive spark was missing still. In terms of published compositions, the year 1906 was the leanest of Joplin's career so far. Only two works were issued, both by Stark from his New York office, and one, *The Ragtime Dance*, was a condensed piano version of the original, a version no doubt intended to recoup some of the losses the Stark concern had sustained as a result of publishing the full-length work. Even the second work, "Antoinette," a conventional 6/8 march, appears stylistically to have been written a year or two before or even earlier. It was a bad time for Joplin, who must have wondered if his compositional ability had left him completely. Why else would he have listed himself in the 1907 St. Louis directory as a laborer?

Yet Scott Joplin soon rose out of his melancholy. The

Scott Joplin, about 1904. This photograph appeared on the cover of "The Cascades" and a drawing from it was included on that of "Euphonic Sounds." *ASCAP*

Louis Chauvin, protégé of Joplin and collaborator with him on "Heliotrope Bouquet." His early death eclipsed a musical genius that many consider might have equaled Joplin's. *New York Public Library*

LEFT, Arthur Marshall, Joplin protégé and collaborator with Joplin on "Swipesy—Cake Walk" and "Lily Queen—A Ragtime Two-Step." This photograph is the one of Marshall that appeared on the cover of "Swipesy." *New York Public Library*

RIGHT, Scott Hayden, Arthur Marshall's friend and fellow protégé of Scott Joplin. It is said that while Joplin and Hayden collaborated on "Sunflower Slow Drag" Joplin courted Hayden's sister, Belle. *New York Public Library*

Joplin introduced James Scott to John Stark and helped him get his first ragtime composition published. Scott would come to be considered second only to Joplin himself as a composer of classic ragtime. *New York Public Library*

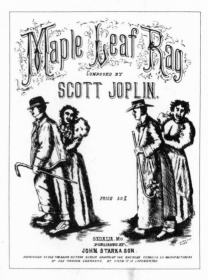

LEFT, The sheet music cover for "Something Doing" (1903), a work by Joplin and Hayden, illustrates the relative positions of blacks and whites in American society at the turn of the century. Note the similarity of the black couple to one of the couples depicted on the original "Maple Leaf Rag" cover. *State Historical Society of Missouri*

RIGHT, The original cover for "Maple Leaf Rag."

Scott and Lottie Joplin's first recorded residence in New York City, 252 West Forty-seventh Street, still standing today. A crumbling old brick building owned by the adjacent Spindletop Restaurant (to the right), it is destined for demolition. *Mesopotamia/Bill Kelly*

Scott Joplin, around 1911. The last known photograph.
Duncan P. Schiedt.

impetus may well have been a trip to New York. White composer Joseph Lamb, ranked in music history with Joplin and James Scott as one of the three "greats" of ragtime, recalls that his first meeting with Joplin occurred in the offices of the Stark Publishing Company at 127 East Twenty-third Street in Manhattan. Lamb was a young, struggling composer who had tried to sell two rags to the Starks, both of which had been rejected. Nevertheless, he was one of the best customers of their sheet music business. He bought so many rags from them that he had a standard discount. On the happy day in 1907 that he met Joplin, he did not recognize the black man sitting in the store talking with Mrs. Stark. Lamb would hardly have noticed him at all if the man had not sported a bandaged foot and a cane. Lamb told Mrs. Stark that he liked the rags of Scott Joplin best and wanted to buy any he did not already have. The stranger spoke up, naming several pieces and asking if Lamb had them. Lamb bought those he did not already own, thanking the stranger for his help. Scott made no attempt to identify himself. As he was leaving, Lamb commented that Scott Joplin was one composer he would like to meet.

"Really," said Mrs. Stark. "Well, here's your man."

Scott learned of Lamb's own attempts to get his rags published and hobbled beside the younger man as they walked along Twenty-third Street. They sat on a bench in Madison Square and talked about the music business. At length, Scott invited the young white man to his home. Eagerly, Lamb went to the boardinghouse where Joplin was staying. When he entered a room filled with blacks, he must have felt some trepidation about his ability to compose works in a musical genre that was identified primarily with blacks. Once he started playing, his fears subsided. Those around him stopped talking to one another and listened; then they approached the piano to watch him. He was playing "Sensation—A Rag," and when he was finished, Joplin paid him a high compliment. "That's a good rag," Scott said, "a regular Negro rag." He offered to present the piece to Stark personally, and to lend his name as arranger (a title which in those days often referred to the one who had arranged to have a piece published).

A week later, Stark offered to buy the piece for twenty-five dollars, with the pledge of another twenty-five dollars after the first printing of one thousand copies was sold. Lamb eagerly accepted and, thanks in large measure to the interest and help of Scott Joplin, the career of Joseph Lamb was launched.[32]

Scott's own career took a decided upturn that year. His creative spark returned, perhaps simply because of the stimulus of the New York environment. Like so many other out-of-towners before and after him, Joplin was awed by New York, and like other newly arrived blacks he was astonished at the city's large black population, which was growing rapidly in that first decade of the twentieth century. Between 1890 and 1910, the black population of New York nearly tripled, and Manhattan received the greatest influx. The majority were from the southern coastal states, and they grouped together, partly out of choice and partly because of residential segregation, in areas like the Tenderloin, Twenty-fourth to Forty-second Streets from Fifth Avenue westward, and Hell's Kitchen. They were mostly poor, mostly young, and mostly unskilled, but there was a largeness about New York and an energy that made anything seem possible, at least for a time.

Eight compositions were published under Joplin's name that year, 1907; two songs, two collaborative works, and four individual pieces. In all probability, the songs were mere potboilers: "Snoring Sampson," with words by Scott's St. Louis newspaper friend Harry La Mertha, and "When Your Hair Is Like the Snow," with lyrics by a man who called himself Owen Spendthrift. Joplin may well have done the music for them in order to earn money to finance his trip from Chicago to New York. Of the two, "Snoring Sampson" is the more interesting. Its "coon cover" depicts a huge-lipped, prickly-headed man snoring loudly while his wife, sporting pickaninny braids that radiate from her head, watches him with extreme displeasure. Subtitled "A Quarrel in Ragtime," the song also has "coon lyrics":

"Samuel Sampson was a coon with a basso voice . . . I tells you that I loves you and I hate to squeal but, I information you this bed's no automobile . . ."

Joplin's arrangement, however, contained a number of original ideas, and his employment of them in the song makes it better musically than the run-of-the-mill ragtime song of the period. Perhaps because of his friendship with La Mertha, Joplin put more effort into the music for this song than he did for the other songs on which he collaborated.

Of the collaborative instrumental works, one was "Heliotrope Bouquet," which Joplin had worked on in Chicago with Louis Chauvin. Sadly, Chauvin was not around to reap the financial or artistic benefits of the collaboration; he died shortly after "Heliotrope Bouquet" was issued. The other collaborative work, "Lily Queen," written with Arthur Marshall while Joplin was in Chicago, appears to contain some Chauvin-like elements (in the third strain) as well. While not as successful artistically as the Joplin-Chauvin collaboration, it is nevertheless a graceful and harmonious work. The Stark Company published "Heliotrope Bouquet," but a new publisher, W. W. Stuart, 48 West Twenty-eighth Street, New York, issued "Lily Queen." Whether Stark rejected the Marshall-Joplin collaboration, or whether Joplin deliberately sought out a new publisher for the piece is not known.

It is likely that Joplin was searching for new publishers. They abounded in New York, and some were interested in publishing works by "The King of Ragtime." Of the four compositions written alone by Joplin issued in 1907, only one was published by Stark, and it is the one of the four that is nearest in style to Joplin's Sedalia-St. Louis period works. "Nonpareil," in fact, might have been written earlier and held by Stark for a year or two before being issued. If so, then Scott did indeed strive toward independence once he arrived in the East.

Two of the 1907 works were published by Jos. W. Stern & Company, 102–104 West Thirty-eighth Street, New York. "Searchlight Rag" was clearly named in honor of the Turpin brothers, who had tried their hand at gold mining in Searchlight, Nevada, years before; its rolling bass calls to mind the rough-and-tumble life of the frontier prospector. The other, "Gladiolus Rag," is true Joplin in its floral title and in its perfect unity. Artistically, it is one of Joplin's most successful rags.

The final individual work published in 1907 was "Rose Leaf Rag," and with "Searchlight Rag" and "Gladiolus Rag" it signals a new stage in Joplin's development and a new meaning for the term "classic rag." In these compositions, ragtime reaches its maturity and becomes not an amalgamation of elements but a unified and highly individual form. Stylistically, there is little question that Joplin composed these works while in New York, or at least after he had left St. Louis. They represent a new era in his career.

"Rose Leaf Rag" was issued by a Boston publisher, Joseph Daly. Scott was moving around a lot at that time. Though he regarded New York as his base, he traveled extensively and did not list himself in the New York City directories. Under the billing "King of Ragtime Composers—Author of *Maple Leaf Rag*," he toured the East Coast during the next few years, and even ventured back into the Midwest, if Jess Williams' recollection is at all accurate.

Williams, an eighty-four-year-old pianist from Lincoln, Nebraska, recalled in 1976 that he was in a musician's clubroom in Lincoln one summer day when a man walked in and identified himself as Scott Joplin. One of the people in the room expressed disbelief, and so to prove his identity Joplin sat down at the piano and played "Maple Leaf Rag" so well that before he was finished everyone in the room knew it had to be the master himself. Joplin, Williams recalls, was in Lincoln to place copies of his rags in the town's music shops on a consignment basis. The teen-age Williams immediately attached himself to Scott, not just because the man was famous and an excellent piano player but because he was attracted to him personally. "You felt as though you could put your trust in him," Williams remembers. Joplin shortly left Lincoln, but he went away leaving Williams with a precious memory and a greater piano-playing repertoire, having taught him the "walking bass" that he has used in his piano playing ever since.[33]

During his travels, Scott visited Washington, D.C.,

where he met Eubie Blake. A native of Baltimore, Blake was then in his mid-twenties and already a veteran ragtime pianist. He had started playing in the Baltimore red-light district at the age of fifteen, sneaking out of his home at night so his mother, who disapproved of ragtime, would not find out. In his late teens he had gone to Washington's substantial red-light district and was firmly ensconced there by the time he met Scott Joplin. "I met Scott Joplin in 1907, '08 or '09," Blake recalled on the occasion of the presentation of *Treemonisha* at Wolf Trap Farm. "I can't remember just which year—oh my, there goes my memory—I met him right here in Washington. He was very ill then and I didn't get to see his greatness, but I remember there was a party for both of us at a colored cabaret."[34]

There Scott also met Lottie Stokes, age thirty-three and five years his junior. Being a spinster, she would not have attracted the average itinerant pianist, but Scott Joplin was not the average itinerant pianist. He was not looking for a passionate love affair; he'd had that and was the worse for it. He was looking for stability, for peace, and for a mature woman who could provide it. Lottie Stokes was that kind of woman. They were married,[35] and Lottie accompanied him in his travels, which now seemed to take on added meaning. They were tours now, not somewhat aimless wanderings. Though the two were often penniless, Lottie was committed to and supportive of Scott. At peace and happy with the love the need for which is infused in so many of his compositions, Scott began to be a productive composer once again.

About that time, he started to write a ragtime instruction manual. He had long been concerned about the "new" style of ragtime piano playing that emphasized speed over correct execution. And the purpose of the manual was to encourage the style he preferred. He also re-emphasized his conviction that ragtime should be accorded respectability as a musical form and that his rags in particular be played and viewed in the manner he wished. The booklet was prefaced with the following "Remarks":

"What is scurrilously called ragtime is an invention that is here to stay. That is now conceded by all classes of musicians. That all publications masquerading under the name of ragtime are not the genuine article will be better known when these exercises are studied. That real ragtime of the higher class is rather difficult to play is a painful truth which most pianists have discovered. Syncopations are no indication of light or trashy music, and to shy bricks at 'hateful ragtime' no longer passes for musical culture. To assist amateur players in giving the 'Joplin Rags' that weird and intoxicating effect intended by the composer is the object of this work."

And so he composed a booklet containing six piano exercises in the "correct" way to play ragtime and called it *The School of Ragtime*. He issued it himself in 1908, and thus became the first black ragtime composer to publish such a manual. (Back in 1897, it will be remembered, white ragtime pianist, Ben Harney had issued *Rag Time Instructor*). Joplin evidently hoped to reach a wide audience with his manual, for he priced it at only fifty cents per copy.

"Sensation—A Rag," Joseph Lamb's first published rag and the one to which Joplin had lent his name as arranger, was issued that year. With it Stark and Lamb would begin a profitable collaboration. Joplin would get no royalties from sales of the sheet music; his intent in lending his name to the piece had been solely to help the young and struggling composer.

Joplin published three rags of his own in 1908, "Fig Leaf Rag," "Sugar Cane," and "Pine Apple Rag." "Fig Leaf Rag" was issued by Stark and, of the three compositions, is the one that harkens back most to his earlier style. However, it contains considerable experimentation, notably a heavily chorded trio and a distinctive choral quality in the final section. Its subtitle, "A High-Class Rag," joins the introduction to *The School of Ragtime* in emphasizing Joplin's concern with the respectability of his compositions.

Having established a good relationship with Seminary Music Company, Joplin published with them the two other rags issued that year. Both reflect his constant experimentation, particularly with choral and songlike qualities. Both are workmanlike in quality. Both sheet music issues contain the standard admonition about not playing the pieces fast as well as an added bit of instruction, a tempo marking $= \, \lrcorner \,$ 100. Curiously, this is a faster tempo than many Joplinophile pianists prefer, and may indicate that at the time Joplin was being influenced toward faster tempos in spite of himself. He departed from his customary behavior in another manner at about that time. Generally described as a modest man and a good but not flashy dresser, Scott may have rather surprised ragtime musician Chauf Williams when he happened to bump into Joplin in New York in 1908. Williams remembers that Joplin was dressed up like a Fancy Dan, and sporting diamonds![36]

Joplin was hard at work on his second opera, the first draft of which he had completed while still in St. Louis.[37]

It was a story about a young black woman on a South-western plantation who attains a position of leadership within the local black community by virtue of her education. He may already have decided to call it *Treemonisha*. Joseph Lamb recalled that Joplin played some of the music for him in New York in 1908 and confided in him his dream of its production.[38]

Unlike the earlier *A Guest of Honor*, Scott did not call this a ragtime opera. It was a folk opera, and evidently he told a lot of other people besides Joseph Lamb about it. The March 5, 1908, issue of the New York *Age* carried in its theater section the following article:

COMPOSER OF RAGTIME NOW WRITING OPERA

Since syncopated music, better known as ragtime, has been in vogue, many Negro writers have gained considerable fame as composers of that style of music. From the white man's standpoint of view he at present is inclined to believe that after writing ragtime the Negro does not figure.

There are many colored writers busily engaged even now in writing operas. Music circles have been stirred recently by the announcement that Scott Joplin, known as the apostle of ragtime, is composing scores for grand opera.

Scott Joplin is a St. Louis product who gained prominence a few years ago by writing "The Maple Leaf Rag," which was the first ragtime instrumental piece to be generally accepted by the public. Last summer he came to New York from St. Louis and it was the opinion of all that his mission was one of placing several of his ragtime compositions on the market. The surprise of the musicians and the publishers can be imagined when Joplin announced that he was writing grand opera and expected to have his scores finished by summer.

From ragtime to grand opera is certainly a big jump—

about as great a jump as from the American Theatre to the Manhattan and the Metropolitan Opera Houses. Yet we believe that the time is not far off when America will have several S. Coleridge Taylors who will prove that the black man can compose other than ragtime music.

The composer is just in his thirties and is very retiring in manner. Critics who have heard a part of his new opera are very optimistic as to its future success.

In his excitement about *Treemonisha,* Scott was able to forget his disappointment over his inability to get his first opera *A Guest of Honor,* produced. Indeed, it is likely that in the face of his hopes for *Treemonisha* he became dissatisfied with the earlier opera, saw it as a merely adequate first attempt at operatic form, and ceased to value it. This seems the only way to explain the fate he allowed to befall *A Guest of Honor.*

In the copyright files in the Library of Congress, on the card for A GUEST OF HONOR, there is a 1905 notation that no copies of the opera had ever been received.[39] Scott Joplin must have been aware of this, for he would have received a copyright notice had the piece reached the Copyright Office.

During his years of traveling before he settled permanently in New York, Scott was frequently short of funds and at times unable to pay his bills. It is said that one time when he could not pay his rent at a Baltimore boardinghouse, he left a trunk full of his possessions with the landlady, intending to reclaim his possessions when he was able to pay the money he owed. He never returned for the trunk.[40] A copy of *A Guest of Honor* may have been in it.

CHAPTER VII

Treemonisha

Scott Joplin and John Stark were having another one of their disagreements. Scott had excitedly talked about *Treemonisha* to Stark, only to be rejected almost out-of-hand. Since the commercial failure of the full-length version of *The Ragtime Dance*, Stark had no interest whatsoever in another lengthy, "high-class" work. Even if he had personally liked *Treemonisha*, he would have been forced to turn down its publication. He simply could not afford it.

Competition within the New York music publishing world was fierce. Between 1900 and 1914 there were nearly a hundred companies in the city publishing ragtime sheet music. And though the former piano and organ peddler was by no means a business novice, his ideas of competitiveness differed somewhat from the New York norm. His were based on hard work and straightforward dealings, not on "slickness." Also to his disadvantage was his deep commitment to classic ragtime in an era when Tin Pan Alley dominated the field in popular music. Years later, his descendants would look back on the businessman Grandpa Stark with some bitterness and criticize him for not being more commercially minded.[1] However, even if he had been shrewder and sharper, and less committed to a particular quality of ragtime music, Stark would have had a hard time making it in New York as a small, independent music publisher.

The music publishing industry was beginning to consolidate, larger companies like Feist and Remick crushing competition from smaller concerns by either buying them out or forcing them out. A price war began, five-and-ten-cent stores like F. W. Woolworth constituting the main offensive front. Larger concerns began to offer their sheet music at reduced prices and to send out pianists to plug their publications in the stores. Small, independent publishing companies could not compete on the same level. The best they could do was to send out protesting flyers to the retail dealers with whom they did business. This is what Stark had to say in one of his circulars:

> Well, it's like this. Some time ago the Whitney Warren Co. (Remick) impatient with the publishing business alone, conceived the idea of appropriating to himself the retail business of the country also. To this end he began buying up stands of the department stores.
>
> Sol Bloom and others followed suit and soon there was a merry war on in retail prices. The "hits" have been persistently sold at 9cts . . . Leo Feist—nettled at seeing a competitor's "hits" going faster than his own filled up the Woolworth 5 and 10ct. stores with music on sale . . . The New York Music Co (Albert Von Tilzer) actually sends a man to these 10ct. stores to sing and push their pieces. It is said that Chas. K. Harris sold Knox 50,000 pieces at one order . . .

No one can tell what the end of this foolish greed will be. Were it not for the copyrights all music would be dragged to the level of cost for paper and printing.

Fortunately, as it is each publisher can only degrade his own publications. We will try to protect the dealer in a profit on our prints and hope we will not be dragged into junk-shop methods. It will be some time yet before our prints are found on sale in barber shops and livery stables.

Though many advertisements were equally verbose in those days, Stark's advertisements were frequently and clearly aimed at a different trade from those of the larger music publishers. He might have done better if he had succumbed to a few gimmicks, but he was not that type of businessman, and in New York if you were not that type of businessman, you lost.

Leo Feist had started out as a small, independent dealer, too, back in 1899, when he had given up the corset business to go into music publishing. But Feist had come up with a gimmick. He created the Feist Band and Orchestra Club, which bands and orchestras could join for a dollar per year and in return receive twelve monthly issues of music, each piece a guaranteed new hit. He advertised heavily in *The Metronome* and before long his club was a huge success. "At the time we were jeered and laughed at, like most great inventors," Feist recalled in 1923. "But the fact that practically every publishing house, especially the popular ones, has an orchestra club today proves that the idea was not ill conceived or carried out." Feist also claimed to have created the "freak title," with the publication of "Smoky Mokes," by Abe Holzmann, another gimmick that attracted the public. John Stark refused to depart from the pretty titles he had traditionally used. Leo Feist prospered; John Stark struggled along.[2]

Added to his commercial difficulties were some grave personal hardships for Stark. His wife, Sarah Ann, was seriously ill, and the medical bills were mounting. Shortly, he would take her back to St. Louis, where she could be cared for by relatives. Stark was a stoic man, but his problems weighed heavily on him and affected his business and personal relationships. Joplin was a sensitive and understanding man, but his concern with his most monumental work overshadowed his awareness of his publisher's difficulties. What eventually brought about a permanent break in the relationship, however, was a purely financial matter.

Early in 1909, beset by financial difficulties, Stark suggested to Joplin that in the future the composer's works be purchased outright rather than on a royalty percentage basis.[3] Since all contracts between the two subsequent to that covering "Maple Leaf Rag" had been verbal ones, in a strictly business sense Stark was not actually remiss in suggesting such an arrangement, but he should have realized what Scott's reaction would be. Naturally, Joplin preferred a royalty arrangement; outright purchases were for struggling new composers. Though he did not receive a substantial amount of money in royalty payments, there was always the possibility of a hit and a sizable profit. No, Scott preferred the old arrangement, and he stood firm in the face of Stark's protestations.

Stark did not take lightly Joplin's refusal of his suggestion. He felt Joplin owed him something for his long years of support for classical, Joplin-style ragtime. He considered the composer ungrateful. A stubborn man, unable to see the other person's viewpoint when his ire was aroused, he vowed not to publish anymore of Joplin's compositions. Angry himself at his publisher's overbearing manner, Scott indicated that was fine with him.

All of Joplin's 1909 publications were issued by Seminary Music Company. It was a productive year for him. No less than six superb piano pieces were issued under his name that year, their very titles attesting to the happiness and peace he had found with Lottie: "Solace—A Mexican Serenade," "Euphonic Sounds," "Pleasant Moments."

"Solace—A Mexican Serenade," is Joplin's only work in tango rhythm, a form not unknown in American music, having been introduced in 1860 with "Souvenir de la Havane" by Louis Moreau Gottschalk. Meant to be played in "very slow march time," it is filled with warmth and with the unmistakable Joplin style, mellowed perhaps by his happy relationship with his second wife. Since the tango form probably originated in Argentina, the adjective "Mexican" likely indicates a searching for a new market. Having traveled across the Atlantic to achieve prominence in England and on the Continent, ragtime was now making inroads south of the U.S. border.

"Wall Street Rag" is a composition that has little to do in mood with its title. Once again its mood is optimistic. Descriptive headings for each of the movements' areas are provided: Panic in Wall Street, Brokers feeling melancholy; Good time coming; Good times have come; Listening to the strains of genuine Negro ragtime, Brokers forget their cares. Yet the headings could have referred to any situation in which hope prevails. Tom Turpin continued to visit New York from time to time, and to see Joplin while he was in town. It is highly possible that Turpin, author of "Harlem Rag" and "Bowery Rag," suggested the title of "Wall Street Rag" to him.

Another of Joplin's 1909 publications, "Pleasant Moments," was a further attempt to produce a ragtime waltz, although it is less experimental than his earlier "Eugenia." This is a gentler waltz, fine to be sure, but not brilliant. The cover depicts a couple in the nostalgic boat on the water situation (in this case a canoe), the man paddling, the woman trailing one hand in the water and holding a parasol in the other. Altogether, a tender and gentle production.

The title of Joplin's fourth 1909 rag, "Country Club Rag," further suggests an urge to the "high class" and genteel. In musical form, it is a mixture of song and ballet and perhaps indicates Joplin's concentration at the time on such forms in *Treemonisha*. Indeed, it has been suggested by one Joplinophile that, had the times and the circumstances been different, Scott Joplin might well have distinguished himself as a composer/choreographer.[4]

The 1909 publications are distinctive in their variety, and "Euphonic Sounds" is no exception. It may well be his most forward-looking piece, for it is a legitimate rag without the customary ragtime stride bass, and indeed, Joplin indicates this departure by subtitling the work "A Syncopated Novelty." "Euphonic Sounds" was considered then and is considered now one of Joplin's finest pieces. James Johnson, who recorded it in 1944, said, "Joplin was a great forerunner. He was fifty years ahead of his time. Even today, who understands 'Euphonic Sounds'? It's really modern."[5] Years later Joshua Rifkin concurred.

The final 1909 rag, "Paragon Rag," has a plantation sound, noteworthy in view of the plantation setting of *Treemonisha*. The second strain introduces the right-hand breaks or lead-ins that would later distinguish the player-piano style of roll-recording players. This second theme also echoes a traditional New Orleans red-light district song, "Bucket's Got a Hole in It—Can't Get No Beer," indicating that, though Joplin had traveled far away from his early days as an itinerant piano player, he had stored away for future use literally everything he had ever heard. His brain was an encyclopedia of folk melodies.

Altogether, the six 1909 compositions form the most stylistically successful group of Joplin pieces. These six alone would have assured him a place in musical annals, for they illustrate the versatility not only of Scott Joplin but also of the rag form. In these compositions, he showed that the rag could be adapted to everything from the waltz to the tango, and, perhaps most importantly in terms of the popular conception of ragtime, could dispense almost entirely with the traditional "oompah" bass and still be a rag.

Yet another rag in which Joplin was involved might have been published that year, a collaboration with Joseph Lamb, who recalled years later, "Scott wrote the first two strains and I wrote the last two and, so far as I recall our talking about it, if someone were told that either of us wrote the whole thing, no one would question it. If, as some people say, we both wrote pretty much alike it was certainly evident in that rag . . . I do not remember the name of the piece we wrote together and I don't even remember how it went. I don't know if he [Joplin] was able to have someone else publish it, but I don't think he tried much because he was beginning to feel kind of low about his trouble with Stark. Stark liked it very much but he was as stubborn as Joplin about their differences and just wouldn't take it."[6]

The May 19, 1910, issue of the New York *Age* carried a Seminary Music Company advertisement for three of the

Joplin rags it had published in the two previous years: "Pine Apple Rag," "Euphonic Sounds," and "Wall Street Rag." Though these rags, and others Joplin had published in 1908–9, were among the finest of his career, they were not selling well, and Seminary Music Company would publish no subsequent Joplin compositions. Indeed, classic ragtime had been all but eclipsed by Tin Pan Alley, and even that highly commercialized form was beginning to decline in popularity. It had become little but cheap trash, and a reaction against it was inevitable. Most of the up and coming young black composers in New York wanted nothing to do with ragtime and looked down on it as low-class Negro music much as many white composers did. They did not distinguish, and in their social insecurity did not care to distinguish, the beautiful and intricate compositions of Joplin, or James Scott or Joseph Lamb, from the hack music that came out of Tin Pan Alley. Men like Scott Joplin thus found themselves composing for an ever-diminishing audience. Their compositions were too difficult for the average parlor pianist and misunderstood by too many of those with the skill to play them.

There must have been times when Scott deeply despaired of the state of ragtime. He had devoted the better part of his life to achieving respectability for the form, and for himself as a purveyor of the form. He had seen ragtime struggle against the tide of public opinion and for a brief time to be carried along by that tide, only to see it thrown back, spit out, and forced to struggle against the tide once more. Had all his efforts been fruitless? There were two paths he could have taken. He could have abandoned ragtime, as most other ragtime professors were doing, and concentrated on more socially acceptable music, which he was certainly capable of writing. Or, he could have stubbornly kept on. He chose the latter course, defiantly refusing to admit he had committed himself to a form that would not make it. His defiance was particularly courageous, for not only did he continue writing classic ragtime, he reached higher. For Scott Joplin, a black man deeply committed to American Negro folk rhythms, to focus his energies on writing the folk opera *Treemonisha* was like W. E. B. Du Bois mounting a serious campaign for the presidency of the United States.

He worked on *Treemonisha* like a man obsessed, despite the paucity of favorable conditions for composing. Unable to live off royalties from the sale of his music, Scott was forced to continue touring. It had been some five years since he had lived a settled life, and though Lottie was supportive and willing to travel with her husband, both she and Scott longed for the stability of a permanent address and a dependable income. They would not settle down for another year or so, and during the year 1910 they lived an essentially hand-to-mouth existence, supported to some extent by Lottie's work as a domestic.[7] Scott published only two compositions in 1910, and one, "Pine Apple Rag-Song," was merely a reissue of an earlier rag to which lyrics had been written by a Tin Pan Alley hack named Joe Snyder. Even as an instrumental, "Pine Apple Rag" had been very songlike, and it is likely that "Pine Apple Rag-Song" was primarily a potboiler intended to make some fast money.

The other composition, "Stoptime Rag," is one of the happiest Joplin ever produced. He may well have written it during a period when work on *Treemonisha* was going well, perhaps after he had completed one of the gay numbers in the opera. It is the *only* post-"Eugenia" Joplin rag in which the by now traditional tempo admonition is missing. Instead, in a rather radical departure, Joplin gives the tempo direction as: "Fast or slow." "Stoptime Rag" also includes this instruction: "To get the desired effect of 'Stoptime' the pianist should stamp the heel of one foot heavily upon the floor, wherever the word 'Stamp' appears in the music," nearly the same instruction as is given in the "stamp" section in both versions of his earlier *The Ragtime Dance*. In "Stoptime Rag," however, the "Stamp" instruction is used throughout, and the song rollicks from beginning to end, an exercise in folk dance that he would perfect in *Treemonisha*. Jos. W. Stern & Company, who published "Stoptime Rag," also copyrighted the piece in Britain and in Mexico, where ragtime was enjoying considerable popularity.

By the end of 1910, Joplin had completed a second draft of *Treemonisha* and was hard at work trying to find a publisher for the book. It proved to be a frustrating task. "What headaches that caused him!" Lottie Joplin recalled years later. "After Scott had finished writing it, and was showing it around, hoping to get it published, someone stole the theme, and made it into a popular song. The number was quite a hit, too, but that didn't do Scott any good."[8]

Somehow, Scott managed to get the money to publish *Treemonisha* under his own imprint, "Scott Joplin Music Pub. Co., New York City, N.Y.," in May 1911. "Treemonisha—an opera in three acts," was 230 pages in length and contained twenty-seven songs. Following is the story, as given in Joplin's own words in the preface:

> The Scene of the Opera is laid on a plantation somewhere in the State of Arkansas, North-east of the Town of Tex-

arkana and three or four miles from the Red River. The plantation being surrounded by a dense forest.

There were several negro families living on the plantation and other families back in the woods.

In order that the reader may better comprehend the story, I will give a few details regarding the Negroes of this plantation from the year 1866 to the year 1884.

The year 1866 finds them in dense ignorance, with no-one to guide them, as the white folks had moved away shortly after the Negroes were set free and had left the plantation in charge of a trustworthy negro servant named Ned.

All of the Negroes, but Ned and his wife Monisha, were superstitious, and believed in conjuring. Monisha, being a woman, was at times impressed by what the more expert conjurers would say.

Ned and Monisha had no children, and they had often prayed that their cabin home might one day be brightened by a child that would be a companion for Monisha when Ned was away from home. They had dreams, too, of educating the child so that when it grew up it could teach the people around them to aspire to something better and higher than superstition and conjuring.

The prayers of Ned and Monisha were answered in a remarkable manner. One morning in the middle of September 1866, Monisha found a baby under a tree that grew in front of her cabin. It proved to be a light-brown-skinned girl about two days old. Monisha took the baby into the cabin, and Ned and she adopted it as their own.

They wanted the child, while growing up, to love them as it would have loved its real parents, so they decided to keep it in ignorance of the manner in which it came to them until old enough to understand. They realized, too, that if the neighbors knew the facts, they would some day tell the child, so, to deceive them, Ned hitched up his mules and, with Monisha and the child, drove over to a family of old friends who lived twenty miles away and whom they had not seen for three years. They told their friends that the child was just a week old.

Ned gave these people six bushels of corn and forty pounds of meat to allow Monisha and the child to stay with them for eight weeks, which Ned thought would benefit the health of Monisha. The friends willingly consented to have her stay with them for that length of time.

Ned went back alone to the plantation and told his old neighbors that Monisha, while visiting some old friends, had become mother of a girl baby.

The neighbors were of course, greatly surprised, but were compelled to believe that Ned's story was true.

At the end of eight weeks Ned took Monisha and the child home and received the congratulations of his neighbors and friends and was delighted to find that his scheme had worked so well.

Monisha, at first, gave her child her own name; but, when the child was three years old she was so fond of playing under the tree where she was found that Monisha gave her the name of Tree-Monisha.

When Treemonisha was seven years old Monisha arranged with a white family that she would do their washing and ironing and Ned would chop their wood if the lady of the house would give Treemonisha an education, the school-house being too far away for the child to attend. The lady consented and as a result Treemonisha was the only educated person in the neighborhood, the other children being still in ignorance on account of their inability to travel so far to school . . .

The opera begins in September 1884. Treemonisha, being eighteen years old, now starts on her career as a teacher and leader.

To summarize the rest of the story, by virtue of her education, Treemonisha represents a threat to Zodzetrick,

the neighborhood conjurer, and his cohorts, Luddud and
Simon. Unable to trick her through conjuration, they kid-
nap her and prepare to throw her into a wasps' nest in the
forest. She is saved just in time by her friend Remus, who
disguises himself as the Devil and frightens the plotters,
who run away.

The other people of the plantation are jubilant at Treemonisha's safe return but vengeful toward Zodzetrick and
his cohorts, who they feel should be punished. But Treemonisha advises forgiveness, and the people come to understand that they have been victims of their own ignorance. They ask her to be their leader, and when she
suggests that the men might not want to follow a woman,
she is assured that they will. The entire community then
celebrates together.

It seems a rather simple and unsophisticated libretto,
yet it deals with an important and profound subject—the
birth and rise of a black leader and the questions of self-
determination and self-government. It can also be viewed
as somewhat autobiographical. It is set near Texarkana
and begins in 1884, when Joplin was still in the town.
Though it is not known whether or not Scott ever had
white teachers, his level of literacy indicates that his own
mother stressed education as Treemonisha's mother did.
And his heroine can be said to reflect his own aspirations
to do for the Negro's music and for black people through
his music what Treemonisha did for her people in leading
them out of ignorance and superstition. Not that he was
egotistical about his mission. His opera is a historical one
in the sense that Treemonisha triumphs over this ignorance and superstition back in the 1880s, more than
twenty years before the opera's publication. By placing
the action at such a time, Joplin is saying, in effect, that

black people have already learned the lesson of *Treemonisha* and are free to determine responsibly their own futures.

Treemonisha was intended as a fantasy with enough reality about it to appeal to the essentially pragmatic American mind; and it is possible that Joplin was influenced by Lewis Carroll, whose *Alice's Adventures in Wonderland* we know he read some years before 1911, for Carroll's works can be read on either a purely fantastic or highly political level. Though he incorporated a number of fantasy elements, such as the huge wasps' nest, the setting is the real world, the words are the Southern black vernacular, and the music is pure American black music.

Though the story may appear naïve to the modern mind, the music is not, and in *Treemonisha*, Joplin achieved what many consider his greatest musical accomplishment, for he synthesized in it all the ragtime forms which he had developed and experimented with throughout his career, while incorporating the ragtime form in a subtle and integrated manner. Musicologists distinguish in the tune "A Real Slow Drag" elements similar to those in Joplin's 1904 composition "The Chrysanthemum" and his 1903 work "Something Doing," in the prelude to Act III of *Treemonisha*, the dotted rhythm pattern in the C strain of the 1906 work "Eugenia," and the upbeat interval of the fourth that is so prominent in "Maple Leaf Rag."[9]

Of the twenty-seven tunes in the opera, two stand out as particularly remarkable—the beginning theme; "Aunt Dinah Has Blowed de Horn," which captures the joy felt by the field workers when "quittin' time" was signaled; and "A Real Slow Drag," the haunting, dude walk melody that closes the opera. But there are many other memorable tunes: the strong and complex "The Bag of Luck," the happy stoptime rhythm of "The Corn-Huskers," the rag-time waltz "Frolic of the Bears," and the comic "We Will Rest Awhile," in the best barbershop quartet tradition.

The music of *Treemonisha* is completely and distinctively American, and it is the first truly American opera, not imitative of the European form. Scott Joplin also choreographed the work. The dancing is as effective in emphasizing the mood as the music is. Here are his "Directions For the Slow Drag":

1. The Slow Drag must begin on the first beat of each measure.
2. When moving forward, drag the left foot; when moving backward, drag the right foot.
3. When moving sideways to right, drag left foot; when moving sideways to left, drag right foot.
4. When prancing, your steps must come on each beat of the measure.
5. When marching and when sliding, your steps must come on the first and third beat of each measure.
6. Hop and skip on second beat of measure. Double the Schottische step to fit the slow music.

In published form, *Treemonisha* was available to anyone who was interested, and the fact that it was reviewed in only one publication should have indicated to Scott that there was not much interest in his opera. The one review, however, was laudatory, and it gave impetus to his stubborn optimism about the work. The review, which appeared in the June 24, 1911, issue of *The American Musician*, was a lengthy one. Following are excerpts:

. . . In literary productivity the colored man has not yet made himself very prominent. The works of Booker T. Washington and Lawrence Dunbar, however, are good examples of the products of the negro mind. In other departments of art the negro has heretofore practically achieved nothing, although his proclivity toward music is universally recognized. It is therefore an occasion for wonderment as well as for admiration when a work of undeniable merit has been wrought by one of this race.

Scott Joplin, well known as a writer of music, and especially of what a certain musician classified as "classic rag-time," has just published an opera in three acts, entitled "Treemonisha," upon which he has been working for the past fifteen years. This achievement is noteworthy for two reasons: First, it is composed by a negro, and second, the subject deals with an important phase of negro life . . . A remarkable point about this work is its evident desire to serve the negro race by exposing two of the great evils which have held this people in its grasp, as well as to point to higher and nobler ideals. Scott Joplin has proved himself a teacher as well as a scholar and an optimist with a mission which has been splendidly performed. Moreover, he has created an entirely new phase of musical art and has produced a thoroughly American opera, dealing with a typical American subject, yet free from all extraneous influence. He has discovered something new because he had confidence in himself and in his mission.

Scott Joplin has not been influenced by his musical studies or by foreign schools. He has created an original type of music in which he employs syncopation in a most artistic and original manner. It is in no sense rag-time, but of that peculiar quality of rhythm which Dvorak used so successfully in the "New World" symphony. The composer has constantly kept in mind his characters and their purpose, and has written music in keeping with his libretto. "Treemonisha" is not grand opera, nor is not light opera; it is what we might call character opera or racial opera. The music is particularly suitable to the individuals concerned, and the ensembles are noteworthy examples of artistic conceptions which conform to the character of the work . . . It is always a pleasure to meet with something new in music. In the many years that we have been associated with printed musical pages, this is the first instance we have observed some wholly strange notations. This composer has employed a very unique method of notating women crying and calls.

There has been much written and printed of late concerning American opera, and the American composers have seized the opportunity of acquainting the world with the fact that they have been able to produce works in this line . . . Now the . . . question is, are the American composers endeavoring to create a school of American opera, or are they simply employing their talents to fashion something suitable for the operatic stage and satisfactory to the operatic management? If so, American opera will always remain a thing in embryo. To date there is no record of even the slightest tendency toward the fashioning of the real American opera, and although this work just completed by one of the Ethiopian race will hardly be accepted as a typical American opera for obvious reasons, nevertheless none can deny that it serves as an opening wedge, since it is in every respect indigenous. It has sprung from our soil practically of its own accord. Its composer has focused his mind upon a single object, and with a nature wholly in sympathy with it has hewn an entirely new form of operatic art. Its production would prove an interesting and potent achievement, and it is to be hoped that sooner or later it will be thus honored.

Such words were "music" to Scott Joplin's ears. What a fine review! How often he read and reread those words of praise from a (white) reviewer in a respected (white) publication, and though there were no more rave reviews, indeed no more reviews at all, Scott proceeded with his plans for *Treemonisha,* an action he probably would have taken had there been no reviews at all.

Joplin had no personal hand in the publishing of the other 1911 work that bears his name, "Felicity Rag," another collaboration with Scott Hayden that John Stark published. In fact, given the state of Joplin's relationship with Stark, it is probable that the rag is one Stark had purchased some years before. Considering Stark's response to Joseph Lamb's collaboration, it is unlikely that he would have purchased "Felicity Rag" subsequent to the break in 1909.

"Felicity Rag" was one of the last works to be published under the label Stark Music Printing and Pub. Co., St. Louis-New York, for shortly thereafter John Stark closed up his New York shop and went back to St. Louis.[10] Competition in New York was too much for an independent company like Stark's, and with the death of his wife in 1910 he found the city an intolerably lonely place. Back in St. Louis, he went to live with his son E.J. and his family, and stubbornly continued to publish classic ragtime compositions from the printing plant "that 'The Maple Leaf Rag' had built."[11] As late as 1916, the Stark company was running ads such as the following:

CLASSIC RAGS
DON'T LET THAT EVER FADE FROM YOUR MEMORY

As Pike's Peak to a mole hill, so are our rag classics to the slush that fills the jobbers bulletins.

As the language of the college graduate in thought and expression to the gibberage of the alley Toot, so are the

Stark rags to the Molly crawl-bottom stuff that is posing under rag names.

This old world rolled around on its axis many long, long years before people learned that it was not flat. Then they wanted to kill the man who discovered it.

St. Louis is the Galileo of classic rags. It is a pity that they did not originate in New York or Paree so that the understudy musicians and camp followers could tip toe and rave about them.

However they still have those Eastern games of wit and virtue "Somebody Else Is Gettin' It Now"—"It Will Never Get Well If You Pick It," etc., etc. Such as these they play over and over ad nauseum—and a bunch of French adjectives.

The brightest minds of all civilized countries, however, have seen the light and are now grading many of the Stark Rags with the finest musical creations of all time.

They cannot be interpreted at sight. They must be studied and practised slowly, and never played fast at any time.

They are stimulating, and when the player begins to get the notes freely the temptation to increase the tempo is almost irresistible. This must be kept in mind continuously. Slow march time or 100 quarter notes to the minute is about right.

When played properly the Stark Rags are the musical advance thought of this age and America's only creation.

CHAPTER VIII

The Last Years

The Joplins finally settled down in late 1911 or early 1912, renting rooms in a boardinghouse at 252 West Forty-seventh Street between Broadway and Eighth Avenue in Manhattan. Scott was listed for the first time in the 1912 city directory as a composer. Forty-seventh and Broadway was the center of Tin Pan Alley in those days. Broadway was literally lined with rows of small music shops, long, narrow establishments each featuring at the front a pianist who played whatever tune a customer wanted to hear. All the latest songs and instruments were clipped onto overhead wires running the length of the store, and the customer walked along the rows of sheet music, reading the titles and making his selections.[1]

Though the area was near the Tenderloin and Hell's Kitchen sections, both of which contained heavy concentrations of blacks, it was not a predominantly black neighborhood. Its many boarding establishments housed the show people, entertainers and musicians who made their living on Broadway and elsewhere in New York's busy entertainment world, transient people who enjoyed a close camaraderie with one another. The Joplin rooms were frequently filled with people, for Lottie was jovial and outgoing and Scott, though rather shy and quiet, enjoyed having around him people who appreciated his kind of music. For their part, the visitors were attracted to both Scott and Lottie. There was always good food and good talk at the Joplins', and Scott did his best to help out his friends whenever he could.

Unfortunately, none of his friends was in a position to give him the help he needed. They were not moneyed people, and they enjoyed no connections with people who were. Though they encouraged him in his efforts to produce *Treemonisha,* they could not help him to realize his dream. He was forced to pound the pavements himself and he did so, tirelessly, for months on end, armed no doubt with copies of the laudatory review that had appeared in *The American Musician,* but becoming increasingly frustrated by the lack of interest in his opera. When he worked, he worked on *Treemonisha,* and he published only a single composition in 1912, "Scott Joplin's New Rag," issued by Stern. A joyful, melodic piece, it may well have been written back in the spring or early summer of 1911, after the score of *Treemonisha* had been published and had received the one glowing review. Interestingly, the tempo instruction is not the usual "Do Not Play This Piece Fast," but is instead "Allegro Moderato," as if to indicate Joplin's view of himself as primarily a composer of opera. The title, too, indicates an ego-involvement not previously seen. It is a fine rag, viewed by some musicologists as being in the "old vein." Perhaps it was a piece that he had roughed out years before.

Certainly Scott was not doing much new composing, not even of potboilers for the sake of ready cash. Scott had apparently sworn off such commercialism; he would make it with *Treemonisha* or he would not make it at all. The small amounts of money he received in royalties and Lottie's earnings working as a domestic maintained a roof over their heads and kept their other creditors at bay. Scott tried to do his part, listing himself in the 1913 city directory not as a composer but as a musician and taking whatever jobs he could find. He also reworked some of the tunes in *Treemonisha,* and in 1913 he published in sheet music form revised versions of two of the numbers, "A Real Slow Drag" and "Prelude to Act 3." Since he published both pieces himself, he put an additional strain on his and Lottie's already meager financial resources.

Money was probably the least of Joplin's worries, however. He was far more disturbed at the decline of ragtime and the attacks on ragtime that were increasing in such publications as the New York *Age.* In April 1913 he wrote to the music editor of that publication a letter that may explain his refusal to do any more potboilers and that definitely states his high opinion of true ragtime:

I have often sat in theatres and listened to beautiful ragtime melodies set to almost vulgar words as a song, and I have wondered why some composers will continue to make the public hate ragtime melodies because the melodies are set to such bad words.

I have often heard people say after they had heard a ragtime song, "I like the music, but I don't like the words." And most people who say that they don't like ragtime have reference to the words and not the music.

If someone were to put vulgar words to a strain of Beethoven's beautiful symphonies, people would begin saying: "I don't like Beethoven's symphonies." So it is with the unwholesome words and not the ragtime melodies that many people hate.

Ragtime rhythm is a syncopation original with the colored people, though many of them are ashamed of it. But the other races throughout the world today are learning to write and make use of ragtime melodies. It is the rage in England today. When composers put decent words to ragtime melodies there will be very little kicking from the public about ragtime.

Barely four months after his letter was published in the *Age*, Scott got his first break, or so it appeared. The following item appeared in the August 7, 1913, issue of the *Age*:

Scott Joplin, the well known composer of ragtime, has interested Benjamin Nibur, manager of the Lafayette Theatre [in Harlem], in the production of his ragtime opera, "Treemonisha." The opera will be produced at the Lafayette in the fall.

By 1913, the area known as Harlem was changing in complexion. The former poor rural community had developed rapidly after the 1870s, when it was annexed by New York City. Older and wealthier New Yorkers had moved to this "residential heaven," whose undeveloped periphery housed poor Italian immigrants and a substantial scattering of blacks (although they were far more disparate in Harlem than in the Tenderloin, for example). What set off the radical alteration of Harlem's population was the construction of new subway routes into the neighborhood in the late 1890s. Speculators quickly bought up all the available Harlem land and property and erected apartment buildings to receive the waves of new people who would move to the area once it had become accessible to downtown Manhattan via the subways. Speculation reached fever pitch, and prices of land and property increased out of all proportion to their actual value. By 1904–5, the subway was nowhere near completion and the speculators realized they were saddled with too many empty buildings and astronomical mortgage payments to the banks. Landlords competed with one another to attract tenants, reducing rental rates or offering other "deals." In desperation, some even began to rent to Negroes, charging them the traditionally higher rentals that Negroes usually paid.

It must have seemed to many of these new Harlemites that the millennium had come. After the squalor of their tenements in the Tenderloin and Hell's Kitchen districts, they were suddenly offered brand new buildings, many of which had not even been occupied before. Harlem proper, with its wide, tree-lined avenues, was a genteel environment, and if its rents were high it was worth scrimping to live there. By 1914, some 50,000 blacks would be living in Harlem, and many of its institutions would integrate.

The Lafayette Theatre, at 2227 Seventh Avenue, was built in 1912 to present white entertainment. The 2,000-seat theater originally had a segregated seating policy, but within a year it had changed to Negro entertainment and desegregated its seating.[2] Joplin's *Treemonisha* was to be one of the first black performances at the Lafayette.

It was August, and if the opera was to open in the fall, Joplin would have to work quickly. The August 14 issue of the *Age* carried the following notice:

Singers wanted at once—call or write Scott Joplin, 252 West 47th Street, New York City. State voice you sing.

But the opera never opened. Perhaps Joplin was unable to get enough performers and rehearse them in time. More likely, the change in plans resulted from a change in the theater's management. The Coleman brothers, who took over that fall, preferred musical comedy offerings, and the show that opened in *Treemonisha*'s stead was a musical comedy production. After coming so close to seeing his dream of a production of *Treemonisha* realized, Scott was plunged into deep despair. For some weeks he was morose, inconsolable.

John Stark brought out Joplin's final collaborative work that year, "Kismet Rag," written with Scott Hayden. As in the case of "Felicity Rag," though Hayden's name appears on the first page, it does not appear on the cover, on which the name "Scott Joplin" alone appears. Also like "Felicity Rag," it appears to be composed of material written some years earlier, but it is more effective. There is a vaudeville quality to it that is infectious. Evidently, Stark, with perhaps some prodding from Hayden, had relented and decided not to maintain his earlier policy of not publishing Joplin compositions. He may have learned of Joplin's difficulties and obsession with *Treemonisha*, or he may simply have decided that publishing Joplin compositions was still good business.

Scott managed to pull himself up out of his depression toward the end of 1913, and his creative spark returned with gusto. Early in 1914 he completed what many consider his finest rag, "Magnetic Rag," which he published himself that same year. It has about it a gentle quality like "The Entertainer," and its distinctive form and range of moods suggest to some musicologists a breakthrough to a Chopinesque form of ragtime, albeit a breakthrough that came too late.[3] He also renewed his efforts to revise various parts of *Treemonisha*, and early the next year he published at his own expense a revised version of "Frolic of the Bears."

In 1915, the Joplins joined the general migration of New York blacks northward to Harlem, renting rooms in a building at 133 West 138th Street.[4] Money was short, and the rent was substantial. To bring in more cash, Scott listed himself in the city directory as a music teacher. His declining fortunes in New York are clearly seen in the city directories. From "Scott Joplin, composer" in 1912–14, he becomes "Scott Joplin, musician" in 1915, and finally "Scott Joplin, music teacher" from 1916 until his death. Encouraged by his friends to keep revising his opera, Scott continued to work on *Treemonisha* and soon his former protégé Sam Patterson arrived in New York to help him.[5]

Since the death of Louis Chauvin in Chicago some years earlier, Patterson had traveled about and had eventually made his way to New York, still the music capital of the country. Meeting up with Joplin again, he urged his old mentor to press on with his work on *Treemonisha*. Joplin confided that he hoped to stage a performance of the opera in order to attract backers, and Patterson agreed to help him with the orchestration. They would work all day, Scott completing pages of the master score, and Sam copying out the various parts. At noon, Lottie would bring them lunch, and they would take a short break before resuming their work. Years later, Patterson recalled a typical lunch:

> Joplin said, "Let's knock off, I hear Lottie coming." Just then the phone rang and I went to answer it. When I came back there were fried eggs on the table and Lottie was opening a bottle of champagne some folks she worked for had given her. I said, "These eggs are cold," and Scott said, "Look, Sam, if they're good hot, they're good cold."[6]

Scott's and Lottie's was a warm and gentle relationship. Though she worried about him, Lottie was always supportive of her husband, and she took great pains to provide a home atmosphere conducive to his work. In return, Scott treated her as the lady she most assuredly was. His last years were replete with disappointments, but they were also the years during which Scott enjoyed his most satisfying personal relationship.

Scott rented the Lincoln Theatre[7] on 135th Street in Harlem for a performance of *Treemonisha* sometime in the early part of 1915, hoping thereby to attract backers for a full-scale production. Quickly, he gathered together a group of young singers and dancers. As Sam Patterson recalled, he "worked like a dog" rehearsing the cast, who were likely working for little or no pay. There was no money for scenery, or costumes, or musicians, and Joplin hoped that the performance would succeed on the merits of its music, songs, and choreography alone. He was wrong. The performance was a flop. The small, mostly invited audience was polite but unenthusiastic. Sitting alone at the piano, playing all the orchestral parts himself, Scott Joplin despaired once again. That night he realized that further attempts on behalf of *Treemonisha* were futile.

Unfortunately, even if *Treemonisha* had been presented as a full production rather than as little more than a preliminary rehearsal, it would probably have not been a success. The Harlem audience, indeed the black New York audience, was not ready for the subject matter of the opera. Many were familiar with opera, and with opera presented by blacks. Black musicians were beginning to get jobs in the opera field. A black singer named Theodore Drury had formed a black troupe and beginning in 1903 presented such operas as *Carmen, Faust,* and *Aida* at the Lexington Opera House.[8] But Southern plantations and black superstitions were too much a part of many black New Yorkers' recent past. Though they could view such subjects objectively, they were not ready to elevate their folk past to the level of art. Their tastes ran to other things, as stated in an article about the Lincoln Theatre that appeared in *The Theatre* magazine in 1916:

> Having experimented with drama of many types, the director has discovered a marked preference for productions permitting the use of drawing rooms and pretty clothes. It is always a great point in a play's favor if the actors, and more especially the actresses, are well dressed. The negro is essentially interested in ladies and gentlemen and has scant sympathy for crooks or Western bandits.[9]

Nor did the whites who witnessed the production, if indeed there were any whites in the audience, see any value in it. Undoubtedly, Scott had invited the critic who had written so glowingly about the published score of *Treemonisha* to attend the performance, but if the man did attend, he did not consider it worth writing about. Not one review, not one word about the performance appeared. Had it been panned, Scott would have had reason to continue fighting for his opera. But it was completely ignored. "American dillettanti," wrote a critic in the London *Times* in 1913, "never did and never will look in the right corners for vital art. A really original artist struggling under their very noses has a small chance of being recognized by them . . . They associate art with Florentine frames, matinee hats and clever talk full of allusions to the dead."[10] Scott could withstand anything, but he could not take silence.

He lapsed into depression once again, but this time he began to exhibit erratic behavior that worried Lottie. He developed strange tics of his facial muscles, began to stumble over difficult words; his handwriting deteriorated alarmingly, and he appeared physically weak. But when Lottie or Sam Patterson or one of his other friends suggested that he seemed tired, he insisted he'd never felt better, and then he would begin to talk excitedly about writing a musical comedy drama, or perhaps a symphony. He was exhibiting the symptoms of dementia paralytica, a disease that is a late manifestation of terminal syphilis.[11]

Having spent their small savings on the ill-fated production of *Treemonisha*, Scott and Lottie were nearly broke, and early in 1916 they moved once again, this time to 163 West 131st Street, where, at Lottie's suggestion, they rented more rooms which she in turn rented out to transients.[12] Rumor has it that some of her boarders were extremely transient, using the place for their one-night stands. Though he appreciated the necessity of running such an enterprise, Scott could not work in that atmosphere. He rented a room two blocks away, at 160 West

133rd Street, where he worked and where he taught his students. But his productivity was minimal. He worked in spurts and, like his young protégé Louis Chauvin before him, seemed unable to complete anything, though he started numerous projects, among them orchestrations of "Stoptime Rag" and "Searchlight Rag" and two new piano pieces, "Pretty Pansy Rag" and "Recitative Rag."[13] He became irritable, undependable. He neglected his students, and one by one they stopped coming.

His mind and his physical dexterity were deteriorating rapidly. He would sit down at the parlor piano and not be able to remember his own compositions. Sometimes, when he tried to compose, his mind went blank. For a number of years, his playing had been inconsistent. Eubie Blake heard him play "Maple Leaf Rag" in 1911 and thought he was terrible. Ragtime musician Dai Vernon had an entirely different impression in 1913. In that year, a friend took Vernon to a publisher's office on Broadway. They found Scott in one of the composing/arranging rooms, playing "Maple Leaf Rag." Vernon remembered that he played it "very, very well—but not too fast. It was in strict time with a positive beat, but it seemed to flow very beautifully. He didn't appear to add any extra notes outside of what were on the music, except that he added an introduction and a fill at the end . . . a nice, quiet fellow, obviously engrossed in his music."[14]

By 1916, however, his playing inconsistency had become even more marked. Pianolas and player pianos had become very popular, and because classic ragtime pieces were too difficult for the average person to play, classic ragtime piano rolls sold particularly well. In April 1916, Joplin recorded several rolls for the Connorized label, among them one of "Maple Leaf Rag" and one of "Magnetic Rag." In June, he recorded "Maple Leaf Rag" again, this time for the Uni-record Melody label. The second version is disorganized, amateurish, a startling departure from the Joplin reputation even as a mediocre player. It is difficult to ascertain whether the difference in these rolls is due to differences in Joplin's playing or to editing on the part of the people at the Connorized company. Though most of the Connorized rolls specifically state "played by Scott Joplin," in the early days of piano rolls the manufacturing companies loved to orchestrate the rolls. The Connorized version of "Maple Leaf Rag" contains some notes that a human could not have played.[15]

Scott still had lucid periods, but they became fewer and were of increasingly shorter duration. During those periods, he worked frenetically at his music, aware, perhaps, that his time was running out. Defiantly, he pursued the extended forms that had played such a crucial role in his demise. In the fall of 1916 he sent the following notice to the New York *Age*, which ran it in the September 7 issue:

> Scott Joplin, the composer, has just completed his music comedy drama "If," and is now writing his Symphony No. 1. He has studied symphonic writing.[16]

Increasingly that fall and winter, however, Scott hadn't the capacity for an emotion as strong as defiance. His emotions and senses were dulled. He felt neither pleasure nor sorrow and he was oblivious to physical pain. On good days, he was preoccupied with the safety of the unfinished manuscripts that littered his desk and piano, and one day in late December 1916 or early January 1917 he burned most of those scripts. Shortly thereafter he descended into the final stage of his disease.[17]

Scott was admitted to Manhattan State Hospital on February 5, 1917.[18] He was so mentally feeble that he could not even recognize the friends who came to visit him. Paralyzed, he lay motionless in his bed, dying slowly from weakness. In the March 29 issue of the New York *Age* there was this brief note:

> Scott Joplin, composer of the Maple Leaf Rag and other syncopated melodies, is a patient at Ward's Island for mental trouble.

Scott died at the age of forty-nine on the evening of April 1,[19] a fitting date, in the cynical view, for the death of a poor, Southern-born black man who had aspired to write opera and to elevate a "low-class" music to the level of symphonic writing. The very month he died, Carl Van Vechten, who would later become such a champion of black culture, wrote in *Vanity Fair* an article praising ragtime as a true American music. However, it was white composers like Louis Hirsch, Irving Berlin, and Lewis F. Muir, whom he singled out for praise. ". . . the best ragtime," he stated, "has not been written by negroes."[20]

"You might say he died of disappointments, his health broken mentally and physically," Lottie Joplin later said of her husband. "But he was a great man, a great man! He wanted to be a real leader. He wanted to free his people from poverty and ignorance, and superstition, just like the heroine of his ragtime opera, 'Treemonisha.' That's why he was so ambitious; that's why he tackled major projects. In fact, that's why he was so far ahead of his time . . .

You know, he would often say that he'd never be appreciated until after he was dead."[21]

A modest funeral was held at the G. O. Paris funeral home at 116 West 131st Street on the afternoon of April 5, 1917,[22] and Scott was buried in a common grave in St. Michael's Cemetery on Long Island. Years before, Scott had made a request: "Play 'Maple Leaf Rag' at my funeral," he had said to Lottie. But when the time came, Lottie decided it just was not appropriate to do so. Years later, she sadly confided, "How many, many times since then I've wished to my heart that I'd said yes."[23]

Eight months later, as a memorial tribute, John Stark issued the last Joplin rag, "Reflection Rag-Syncopated Musings." Some musicologists feel it is one of his most classical and most beautiful. Others believe it was a piece that Stark had kept in his files for some time, and consider it so untypical of Joplin that its attribution is questionable. What is important is the intent of the publication, for despite their differences Joplin and Stark had enjoyed a high respect for each other. "Here is the genius," wrote Stark, "whose spirit . . . was filtered through thousands of . . . vain imitations."[24]

NOTES

Because the notes in this book are so extensive, I have omitted many that refer simply to city directories of Texarkana, Sedalia, St. Louis, Chicago, and New York for various years. Published yearly, or less frequently depending on the size of the town, in the days before telephone books these directories functioned to locate and identify the citizens of an area. As research sources they are invaluable, and far more helpful than modern telephone books, for they list occupations and often indicate ownership, or lack thereof, of the premises occupied. These directories helped to establish the residences, and in some cases the very presence, of Joplin and others in various towns and cities at different times, including the fact that Joplin never owned any of the homes in which he lived, which belies Joplin legend.

PROLOGUE: *The Rediscovery of Scott Joplin*

1. Interview with Fred Joplin by Dick Reavis, June 1976.
2. Ibid.

3. Taped correspondence from Jerry Atkins, June 1976.

4. Ann and John Vanderlee. "The Early Life of Scott Joplin," *Rag Times*, January 1974, p. 2; telephone conversation with Charles Steger, August 13, 1976 (Steger has a copy of Monroe's death certificate).

5. Death certificate, Jiles Joplin, State of Arkansas State Board of Health, Bureau of Vital Statistics; the spelling of Jiles Joplin's name is discussed in Note 6 of Chapter I.

6. Ethel Brown and Donita Fowler are now living in California.

7. She did not own these buildings, according to records in the New York City Municipal Reference Library.

8. Kay C. Thompson. "Lottie Joplin," *The Record Changer*, October 1950, p. 18.

9. S. Brunson Campbell. "The Ragtime Kid (An Autobiography)." *Jazz Report*, VI, 1967, n.p.

10. R. J. Carew. "Treemonisha," *The Record Changer*, October 1946, p. 17.

11. James Lincoln Collier. "The Scott Joplin Rag," New York *Times Magazine*, September 21, 1975, p. 28.

12. Reprinted in "Ragtime Gets Boost into Musical 400," *Rag Times*, March 1972, p. 10.

13. *Rag Times*, September 1974, p. 5.

14. Dick Zimmerman. "Sedalia Rediscovers Ragtime," *Rag Times*, November 1968, p. 13.

15. "School Named for Scott Joplin," New York *Amsterdam News*, February 8, 1975, p. D-11.

16. For some years the rumor persisted that a copy of the opera was in Nevada City, California, in the safe of a Mr. Ott, a former county assayer. However, in 1976 Joplinophile Robert Bradford tracked down the rumor and proved it false. Though the safe contained handwritten manuscripts, they were songs, dated 1865–90, and definitely not by Scott Joplin. Robert Bradford, "In Search of the Guest of Honor," *Rag Times*, May 1976, p. 3.

17. "Rare Rag Roll Found," *Rag Times*, May 1970, p. 1; " 'Silver Swan Rag' Now Available," *Rag Times*, March 1973, p. 2.

18. "Joplin Song Discovered!," *Rag Times*, May 1977, p. 7.

19. James Lincoln Collier, op. cit., p. 33.
20. Solomon Goodman. "Lottie Joplin," *Rag Times*, September 1976, p. 3. Nor did she reap the monetary benefits of the Joplin revival. Whatever royalties, cash awards, etc., that have been paid have gone to her heirs, and it is doubtful that these sums are extensive, since copyrights on most of Joplin's compositions have run out. Joplin's surviving blood heirs, notably his niece, Donita Fowler, have inquired about money accrued to his estate, but under New York law none of the nieces and nephews is entitled to royalties from the music still under copyright. The Surrogate's Court, County of New York, made a search of its records at the request of this author and confirmed that Joplin left no will.

CHAPTER I: *Prelude*

1. Nancy Moores Watts Jennings. "Moores or Mooresville and Harrison Chapel Cemetery, Bowie County, Texas." The area was located about eight miles west of present day Texarkana. For purposes of clarity, it will be called Mooresville here. Most of this section on the early history of the Moores in Texas is indebted to Mrs. Jennings' history.
2. Emma Lou Meadows. "De Kalb and Bowie County History and Genealogy." Trammels Trace was named for Nicholas Trammel, who earlier in the century had made a business of running stolen slaves and horses from Arkansas to Texas. He made deals with the slaves whereby after they were resold in Texas they would run away and return to him, to be sold again.
3. Nancy Moores Watts Jennings, "Moores or Mooresville and Harrison Chapel Cemetery, Bowie County, Texas," n.p.
4. Ibid. According to Mrs. Jennings, other regiments camped at Mooresville on the way to Mexico during the war, indicating that Colonel Charles Moores was in or closely associated with the militia.
5. Interview with Mrs. Jennings by Dick Reavis, June 1976.
6. In earlier books on Joplin, his father's name is spelled

with a "G," and he is listed under that spelling in the 1880 Bowie County census. However, the 1850 slave census gives the "J" spelling, as does Jiles Joplin's death certificate. Texarkana city directories carry different spellings in different years (Giles in the 1899–1900 and 1922 editions, Jiles in the 1906 edition). The "J" spelling is used here throughout.

7. 1850 Bowie County Slave Census, National Archives Micro Copy No. T-6, Roll No. 317. This is an exciting recent discovery, made by Mrs. Arthur Jennings. Benjamin Booth is a researcher's and historian's hero, for this Bowie County census seems to have been the only one to include the names of slaves and is thus an invaluable source. Who was Benjamin Booth and what was his motive in recording the slaves names? Although it is interesting to speculate on his attitude toward slavery, the answer is probably that Booth was a man with an eye for detail and who felt that a census was not complete unless it listed names, whether or not space was provided for this purpose. Presuming, as this author does, that the Jiles listed here is Jiles Joplin, we might never have been able to trace him if not for this census.

There is no proof that Jiles, slave of Charles Moores, was Jiles Joplin, father of Scott Joplin. However, the presence of a small slave named Jiles in the Red River area of East Texas helps to explain how Jiles Joplin, listed as having been born in North Carolina in the 1870 and 1880 federal censuses as well as on his death certificate, managed to get to Texas. Earlier books on Joplin state that Jiles was freed in North Carolina and then traveled to Texas. However, it is difficult to imagine his choosing to make his way to Texas through the South in the years before the war, for he would have been in danger of being captured as a runaway and/or re-enslaved. Also, between 1836 and 1865 a special act of the Texas state legislature was necessary for a freed slave to be allowed to remain in the state and, presumably, to enter the state. No freed slave named Jiles was the subject of such a special act. (Letter from Jean Carefoot, reference archivist, Texas State Library, September 1, 1976.) No legislation regarding free blacks mentions a Joplin, nor do any of the memorials and petitions to the legislature in that period. Jiles may have been purchased from somewhere in North Carolina by James Rochelle.

8. The 1870 federal census gives Jiles's age as twenty-eight; the 1880 census as thirty-eight; his death certificate does not give an exact age.

9. Interview with Mrs. Arthur Jennings, June 1976; the 1860 slave census lists a D. W. Rochelle as holding ten slaves in trust for John Ross Rochelle, who had not yet reached the age of maturity. Also, Henry Rochelle is listed as owning sixteen slaves. Since no slave names were given in this census, we do not know if Jiles was among these twenty-six.

10. All earlier sources on Joplin state that Jiles had been trained in the European musical tradition and had played the violin at plantation dances. Most of these books are based on *They All Played Ragtime,* by Rudi Blesh and Harriet Janis, who obtained much of their information from interviews with Lottie Stokes Joplin among others. Presumably this is where the information on Jiles's musical ability originated. It is supported to some extent by Mrs. Jennings' research into the Moores family history and her visits to the Moores home before it was torn down.

11. Genealogy compiled by Mrs. Arthur Jennings on the occasion of the dedication of the Hooks Town Marker. Hooks still exists as a town today, with a population of less than two hundred.

12. The 1860 census lists Warren Hooks as having ninety-one slaves.

13. Hooks genealogy. The date of the marriage is not known. The 1870 census shows Josiah and Minerva B. Joplin living in the household of her father, Warren Hooks. The Joplins are listed as having two children, ages three and one. However, since Minerva was born in 1843 and it was customary for women to marry young, she was probably married in the late 1850s. Earlier children may have died. Once again, the connection with Jiles is conjectural, but

since Josiah Joplin was the only Joplin in the Red River area at the time, it is likely that he was Jiles's last master and thus the man whose name Jiles took as his own.

14. Given the laws prohibiting freedmen, one wonders how he managed to travel about in the state. It is probable that the laws were not strictly enforced.

15. Unfortunately, information on Florence's early life—even information on which to base speculations—is sparse. Mattie Harris, Scott's niece, recalled that her grandmother's family were overseers of slaves. Fred Joplin, Scott's nephew, believes that only his grandfather was born in slavery. Scott Joplin must have told his wife, Lottie, that his mother was freeborn, for this information is contained in the Blesh and Janis book. The condition of birth of ancestors is very important in black family histories, and it is difficult to discount the recollections of the surviving members of the Joplin family. All attempts at locating Florence in Kentucky censuses have failed.

16. That Florence's father was Milton Givins and her grandmother Susan Givins is conjectural, based on the 1870 census, which shows the Joplins living on the property of a family named Caves along with a Milton Givins, age fifty, from Kentucky, the same state in which Florence was born, and a Susan Givins, age seventy.

As to the Givinses being free, once again there is the problem of the legislation regarding admission of free blacks to the state. No Givinses were the subjects of any special acts. There was a slaveowner named J. W. Givins in the area of present-day Linden, but none of the ages of his slaves given in the 1860 census are even close to those of Milton or Susan, so no connection can be made. The lack of records makes the truth difficult to ascertain, but perhaps someday someone will find a document or documents that will establish Florence Givins' background and give a clue to the circumstances under which she and Jiles met.

17. Ann and John Vanderlee, "Scott Joplin's Childhood Days in Texarkana," *Rag Times*, November 1973, p. 6. Zenobia Campbell is now deceased.

18. The 1870 census lists Monroe's age as seven, the 1880 census gives his age as nineteen and is probably more accurate.

19. Green C. Duncan Papers, University of Texas Archives, letter from Green C. Duncan to Mrs. M. E. Duncan, December 3, 1865.

20. It is not known when Jiles and Florence arrived on the Caves property, only that they were there in 1870. There is no Caves listed in the 1860 census.

21. S. Brunson Campbell and Roy Carew gave this date in one of their 1945 articles in *The Record Changer.* Blesh and Janis later used it in their book *They All Played Ragtime* and presumably had verified it with Joplin's widow, Lottie.

22. There has been some controversy over Joplin's birthplace. Alexander Ford, now deceased, told Ann and John Vanderlee in 1959 that the Joplins had lived near Marshall, Texas, when the Fords had lived there, leading to the speculation that Scott might have been born near Marshall. Most earlier books on Joplin give his birthplace as Texarkana, where he had grown up, to save time and needless explanation.

    Scott Joplin himself probably contributed to the confusion. After he left Texas and traveled to cities like St. Louis and New York, it is likely that he gave his birthplace as Texarkana, where he had grown up to save time and needless explanation.

23. Henry Lee Swint. *The Northern Teacher in the South,* p. 130.

24. Dorothy Sterling. *The Trouble They Seen: Black People Tell the Story of Reconstruction,* p. vii.

25. This is undocumented. Fred Joplin, Monroe's son, stated in June 1976 that his grandfather, Jiles Joplin, always said the family went to Texarkana from Jefferson. Mrs. Mattie Harris, Monroe's daughter, said that Jefferson was often mentioned in family conversations. However, Jiles and Florence may simply have identified with the largest

nearby town and at the time Jefferson was the largest town in the area near present-day Linden.

26. It is not known when the move occurred. The possibility must be reiterated that the Joplins also lived near Marshall, Texas, at some point before going to Texarkana. Old Joplin family friend Alexander Ford told the Vanderlees that the Joplins moved to Texarkana "soon after the birth of the youngest child." Since the youngest Joplin child, Myrtle, is listed in the June 1880 census as three months old, the family might have just arrived in Texarkana. However, Arthur Marshall's recollections are somewhat suspect. Elderly Texarkana resident George Mosley and a man named Burl Mitchell, who was Alexander Ford's best friend, as well as Ford's nephew Alec, say Ford did not come from Marshall. Also Fred Joplin says his *mother's* people came from Marshall; thus, Ford may have the families confused.

CHAPTER II: *Texarkana*

1. "History of Texarkana, Texas," pamphlet (New York Public Library), p. 2.
2. Barbara Overton Chandler and J. Ed. Howe. "History of Texarkana and Bowie and Miller Counties, Texas-Arkansas," p. 8; "History of Texarkana, Texas," p. 2.
3. Nancy Moores Watts Jennings, "Moores or Mooresville and Harrison Chapel Cemetery, Bowie County, Texas," n.p.
4. The Bowie County, Texas, census of 1880, lists Jiles as a "common laborer."
5. Nancy Moores Watts Jennings and Mary L. S. Phillips, compilers. "Texarkana Centennial Historical Program," p. 9; Nancy Moores Watts Jennings, op. cit., n.p.
6. Nancy Moores Watts Jennings and Mary L. S. Phillips, op. cit., p. 9.
7. There are no records of where the Joplins lived on the Texas side, only that they were living on the Texas side as of June 1880, when the federal census was taken. Mrs. Arthur Jennings, of the Bowie County Historical Commis-

sion, feels that the census taker may have moved west along the side streets starting from State Line Avenue. The Joplins are entry number 261 on the census and W. R. Hooks is number 264. In 1897, W. R. Hooks's widow was living at 803 Pine Street, leading to the conjecture that the Joplins also lived on Pine, a block or so east of the Hookses. The first black church in Texarkana, Mt. Zion, was erected in 1875 on the Texas side, at Fourth and Elm, not far from where the Joplins might have lived.

8. Subsequent to the 1870 census, for she is not listed on it. There is some confusion about the spelling of her name. The 1880 census lists her as Josie, age ten; the 1899–1900 city directory lists her as Osie; some interviewees say her name was Ocie.
9. People of all races comprised the bucket brigades. There were black fire-fighting companies in towns like Marshall and Columbus.
10. Edward King. *The Great South,* p. 99.
11. Recently some contradictory theories have been advanced regarding the attitudes of the immigrants to the freedmen they encountered in the West, but most historians agree that there was considerable antiblack sentiment among the white newcomers and that their competition for jobs and land rendered blacks' economic situation even more perilous than it was already.
12. The 1880 census lists both Scott and Robert as "Going to school."
13. Henry Allen Bullock. *A History of Negro Education in the South,* p. 27.
14. William R. Davis. *The Development and Present Status of Negro Education in East Texas,* p. 26.
15. This information is contained in earlier Joplin books and presumably was obtained from Lottie Stokes Joplin by Blesh and Janis. There is little reason to dispute Jiles and Florence Joplin's musical interests, for all but the eldest Joplin child later sang or played instruments.
16. Jim Haskins and Hugh F. Butts. *The Psychology of Black Language,* p. 68.

17. W. F. Allen, C. P. Ware, and L. M. Garrison. *Slave Songs of the United States,* p. 89.

18. Jim Haskins and Hugh F. Butts, op. cit., pp. 68–69.

19. J. M. Carroll. *A History of Texas Baptists,* p. 337.

20. James Haskins. *Witchcraft, Mysticism and Magic in the Black World,* p. 109.

21. A history of the black community in Texarkana compiled by the students of Dunbar High School in 1939. Hereafter, it will be referred to as "The 1939 History": ". . . the members on the Arkansas side all had to go down to Mt. Zion to worship."

22. Lawrence D. Rice. *The Negro in Texas: 1874–1900,* p. 274.

23. Jim Haskins and Hugh F. Butts, op. cit., p. 73.

24. *The Nation,* Vol. 4, May 30, 1867, pp. 432–33.

25. Marshall W. Stearns. *The Story of Jazz,* p. 128.

26. Interview with George Mosley by Dick J. Reavis, June 1976. Mag Washington, incidentally, was George Mosley's aunt.

27. Records of a real estate transaction in 1897 list him as Professor J. C. Johnson.

28. Interview, June 1976. Over the years there have been attempts to identify sites that might have served as the model for the plantation in *Treemonisha.* In 1889 Wesley and Mary Johnson, presumably relatives of J.C., made him "agent and attorney in fact" for them for twelve acres of rural land they owned in Miller County, Arkansas. Dick J. Reavis identified the tract as four miles north of the center of Texarkana in the area now called Sugar Hill. While the Johnson couple did not purchase the acreage until September 12, 1887, it is possible that they had worked the land for years before buying it. It is interesting to imagine Scott, while under the influence of J. C. Johnson, traveling with him to the area to visit his teacher's relatives and later recalling the site and using it as his setting for *Treemonisha.*

29. Listed as three twelfths of a month old in the 1880 census and, inexplicably, as a male child named Johnny.

30. The 1880 census for Bowie County lists numerous cases of

measles among black children in Texarkana, Texas, including Osie, Willie, and Myrtle.

31. Interview, June 1976.
32. They were living together when the 1880 census was taken in June of that year. Alexander Ford, interviewed by the Vanderlees in 1959, said that Scott was about twelve when the separation occurred. Eugene Cook, for whose mother Florence Joplin worked, described her to the Vanderlees as a widow and said Scott was twelve or thirteen years old when Florence worked at the Cook home. Earlier Joplin sources state that one reason for the separation was Florence's purchase of a piano for Scott, but it is doubtful that she purchased one at this time, for later Scott practiced on the Cooks' piano.
33. The 1880 census lists her occupation as "Wash & Iron."
34. This is the earliest Joplin residence in Texarkana of which there is any record, and that record is a late one, contained in the 1899–1900 city directory. However, all the Texarkanans interviewed agree that Florence and her children were living there after Jiles and Florence separated. The house was located on what property records designate as Lots 10, 11, or 12 of Block 26 of the original townsite of Texarkana, Arkansas. A search of property records reveals no Joplin ownership.
35. Interview with George Mosley, June 1976; "The 1939 History," op. cit.
36. Interview with Fred Joplin, June 1976.
37. "The 1939 History." George Mosley says that this is where the church was when he was born in 1887.
38. Florence is described as caretaker of a church in Rudi Blesh and Harriet Janis, *They All Played Ragtime.* George Mosley remembers her ringing the bell of the Canaan Baptist Church after it was formally established. That she acted as caretaker while it was housed in the Dyckman Hide house is conjecture.
39. Ann and John Vanderlee, "The Early Life of Scott Joplin," *Rag Times,* January 1974, p. 2.
40. R. J. Carew and Private Don E. Fowler. "Scott Joplin:

Overlooked Genius," *The Record Changer*, October 1944, p. 11.

41. The Texas Gazetteer and Business Directory 1882–83, Standard Directory Service for Texarkana, says "good public schools." Fred Joplin, Monroe's son, states, "My father didn't go to school."

42. Fred Joplin states that he skipped five grades of school. "I went from the sixth grade to the eleventh, and graduated."

43. "The 1939 History" (p. 4) makes this statement about the later Orr School, and it is assumed there were none at Central High, which was later called Dunbar High School.

44. Until recently, Orr School was regarded as the first school for blacks in Texarkana. There is considerable evidence, although no formal records exist, that Central High School existed well in advance of Orr School. "The 1939 History" devotes a paragraph to it. More compelling evidence is contained in the "First Annual Report of Public Free Schools of City of Texarkana, Tex., 1886–87," which includes a synopsis of a report "From the Principal of Colored School to Superintendent": "Enrollment 198 over 147 the year before and 96 in 1885 . . . A suitable building is a crying necessity . . . a High School Department imminent in two more years . . ." According to the dates mentioned in this report, there was indeed a black school of some sort operating as early as 1885 and perhaps earlier. The same report from the principal of the "Colored School" also mentions another school: "I suggest the schools be united; I speak of the School near Bowie Lumber Co.'s mill, under the charge of Mr. Sims . . ." "The 1939 History" mentions no Mr. Sims. Mrs. Jennings has tried to document, at my request, the location of the mill but has found only a Stevens Brick Yard on Congress Avenue about 1880–1900 not far from Dickey Clay Pipe, which was formerly a lumberyard.

45. Presumably, Lottie Joplin told this to Blesh and Janis; there is no documentation.

46. Interview with George Mosley, 1976.

47. Ann and John Vanderlee, op. cit., p. 3.
48. Ibid.
49. Ibid.
50. Ibid. The Orr School building exists today as a one-story structure, Twin-City Day Care Center.
51. Ibid. Other Joplin sources state that the group was formed during Joplin's Sedalia period. Although Ford's credibility is questionable in some respects, it is likely that Joplin formed such a group when he was a teenager and that he revived it later during his days in Sedalia.
52. Most Joplin sources state that Scott left the town when he was fourteen, after the death of his mother. However, Florence Joplin did not die until 1902 or 1904. In a 1945 article, S. Brunson Campbell and Roy J. Carew stated that Scott left Texarkana at about the age of twenty; Zenobia Campbell says she was at Orr School with Scott; and dates and facts concerning his stay in St. Louis also point to a considerably later date for his leaving home.

CHAPTER III: *Itinerant Pianist*

1. S. Brunson Campbell. "The Ragtime Kid (An Autobiography)" (unpublished), Fisk University Library Special Collections, Samuel Brunson Campbell Papers, n.p.
2. This is the most widely accepted explanation of the derivation of the term *ragtime*, although there are many others. Here are two more. It was born on the levees of the Mississippi in the 1880s, where children in ragged or tattered garments danced to the music played by itinerant black pianists, leading to the identification of the music as ragtime. It arose in the saloons of Louisiana, where white pianist Ben Harney, who later published several ragtime compositions, was frequently greeted with the words, "Take off your rag and play us those new songs." In time, when Harney would arrive, the boys would say, "It's ragtime," in anticipation of the music he would play. "How Did Ragtime Get Its Name?," *Rag Times,* September 1976, p. 8.

3. In 1970 this author visited the Sea Islands of South Carolina, whose native black population, called Geechee, have been isolated for centuries and thus have retained a number of Africanisms. Attending a church service, I heard the combination sorrowful melody/staccato clapping described in these pages, and even to this ear, accustomed to syncopation in a variety of forms, it was a strange and almost incomprehensible sound.

4. Marshall W. Stearns. *The Story of Jazz*, p. 111.

5. Ibid., pp. 111–12.

6. No doubt this is the origin of the later personification of segregation in the character of Jim Crow.

7. Alain Locke. *The Negro and His Music: Negro Art Past and Present*, p. 54; selected from *The American Negro: His History and Literature*, William Loren Katz, general editor.

8. Addison Walker Reed. *The Life and Works of Scott Joplin*, pp. 174–75.

9. Bernard Katz, ed. *The Social Implications of Early Negro Music in the United States*, p. 13; selected from *The American Negro: His History and Literature*, William Loren Katz, general editor.

10. Ibid., p. xi.

11. Addison Walker Reed, op. cit., p. 175.

12. Ibid., pp. 175–76.

13. William J. Schafer and Johannes Reidel. *The Art of Ragtime*, p. 8.

14. Ibid., p. 6.

15. S. Brunson Campbell, "The Ragtime Kid (An Autobiography)" *Jazz Report*, VI, 1967, n.p.

16. Lillian Brandt. "The Negroes of St. Louis." American Statistical Association, New Series No. 61.

17. S. Brunson Campbell. "A Hop Head's Dream of Paradise," unpublished, Fisk University Library Special Collections, Samuel Brunson Campbell Papers, n.p.

18. According to legend, Joplin arrived in St. Louis in 1885 and immediately began to frequent the Silver Dollar Sa-

loon, which John L. Turpin was running by himself as his *two* sons were off on a mining expedition in Searchlight, Nevada. John L. Turpin appears to have had three sons, Robert, Thomas, and Charles. Charles and Thomas were mining in Searchlight, Nevada, in 1881, and they may indeed have been there still in 1885, for there is no listing for them in 1885 or 1886; nor, for that matter, are there listings for John L. Turpin for these two years. In 1887 John L. and Charles Turpin, laborer and bellhop respectively, are listed as rooming at 8 Moore. In 1888, Charles, laborer, is rooming at 4172 New Manchester Road and John L., "roots," is rooming at 1422 Market. In 1889 there is no listing for Charles, and John L. is listed under no occupation, still rooming at 1422 Market. The 1890 city directory is the first to list John L. Turpin's saloon at 425 South Twelfth Street. He is still rooming at 1422 Market and in this year he is joined at this address by Charles, Robert, and Thomas, all of whom are listed as bartenders. In 1891, all are rooming at 1422 Market, Robert and Charles are listed as bartenders, and Thomas is now given the listing "music." It is more likely, then, that the Silver Dollar Saloon was established in 1890 and all three sons were in St. Louis at the time, *and* that Joplin arrived in the city considerably later than 1885.

19. Rudi Blesh. "Scott Joplin: Black American Classicist," Introduction to *Scott Joplin: Collected Piano Works,* Vera Brodsky Lawrence, ed., p. xxxi.
20. Interview with Jan Goldberg, May 1976.
21. Addison Walker Reed, op. cit., p. 20. This trip of Joplin's to Chicago and his activities there are all based on legend, as there is no real documentation of his stay. In fact, his only documented stay in the city occurred in 1905–6.
22. Ibid., p. 22.
23. There is no documentary evidence that Joplin was in Sedalia at this time, but it may explain how Emmett Cook became part of the revived Texas Medley Quartette, for Cook was based in Sedalia.
24. Alexander Ford told the Vanderlees that Scott came back

frequently between engagements and taught guitar, mandolin, and piano during his visits to Texarkana.

25. Ann and John Vanderlee, "The Early Life of Scott Joplin," *Rag Times,* January 1974, p. 3.

26. It is also possible, of course, that Joplin merely mailed his compositions to Syracuse and never performed there. But it is more likely that he peddled his music personally, for he was an unknown composer.

27. Roy Carew and Private Don E. Fowler. "Scott Joplin: Overlooked Genius," *The Record Changer,* September 1944, p. 14.

28. S. Brunson Campbell and R. J. Carew. "Sedalia, Missouri: Cradle of Ragtime," *The Record Changer,* June 1945, p. 3.

29. According to the sheet music cover, Smith was an agent for the London firm of Chas. Sheard & Co., but no registration for the work has ever been found in the London copyright office. It is customary for a composer's previous works to be listed on the cover, but there is no mention of Joplin's two songs published the previous year. Perhaps they were left out because they were songs and this was an instrumental piece.

30. Addison Walker Reed, in *The Life and Works of Scott Joplin* (p. 68), feels that the only one of the three compositions to include syncopation is "Harmony Club Waltz," specifically in the fifth strain. In any case, the intensive study of the development of ragtime elements in Joplin's music may have caused musicologists to stretch the point a bit and find echoes of a syncopation that is not actually there. In the absence of any recordings of these works by Joplin, the point remains debatable. Incidentally, the first page of "Great Crush Collision March" contains the blurb "Scott Joplin, Author of 'Combination March,' 'Harmony Club Waltz,' &c." and presumably the "&c" refers to his two published songs. However, it is possible that not all of Joplin's works have been accounted for and that there may be an early march or waltz yet to be discovered.

31. Campbell states that Saunders accompanied Joplin on the Texas Medley Quartette tour. "From Rags to Ragtime and

Riches," unpublished, Fisk University Library Special Collections, Samuel Brunson Campbell Papers, n.p.

CHAPTER IV: *Sedalia*

1. "Cape Girardeau," *Rag Times,* September 1975, p. 2.
2. S. Brunson Campbell and R. J. Carew. "Sedalia, Missouri: Cradle of Ragtime," *The Record Changer,* May 1945, p. 26.
3. Addison Walker Reed, op. cit., p. 23. Reed interviewed an Ida Mae Abbott of Sedalia regarding the teachers under whom Joplin might have studied at the college, which was destroyed by fire in April 1925. No records exist to attest to the dates of Joplin's enrollment or the courses he took.
4. A native of Leavenworth, Kansas, Daniels was at the time employed by Hoffman as a song plugger and arranger with E. Harry Kelly. Under the name Neil Moret, Daniels would later write "Hiawatha," which he sold to Whitney Warner for $10,000. Dennis Pash. "E. Harry Kelly," *Rag Times,* March 1976, p. 2.
5. The article is presented in full later in the chapter.
6. S. Brunson Campbell. "Ragtime Begins: Early Days with Scott Joplin Recalled," *The Record Changer,* March 1948, p. 8.
7. In a letter to Arna Bontemps among the Samuel Brunson Campbell Papers at Fisk University, Tom Ireland, who played clarinet in Joplin's band, states that Joplin did not particularly like band music.
8. "Ragtime Music Was Born in Sedalia," Sedalia *Democrat,* October 16, 1960, p. 10.
9. S. Brunson Campbell and R. J. Carew, op. cit., p. 36. The authors also say that the owner of this tavern, which they do not identify, was among those who encouraged Joplin to enroll in the Smith College of Music. As mentioned earlier in the text, Campbell identified a black tavern operator as influential in Joplin's enrollment. It is possible that the two sources are actually referring to the same club, the different racial identification of the owner notwithstanding.

213

10. S. Brunson Campbell, op. cit., p. 8. The Black 400 Club is not listed in any Sedalia city directories.

11. "The Original Maple Leaf Club," *Rag Times*, May 1974, p. 3. Other Joplin sources do not appear to have noted or given sufficient attention to Campbell's references to this club and seem to have concentrated almost exclusively on the Maple Leaf Club. Yet, as will be seen, it is doubtful that the Maple Leaf Club existed before 1899.

12. S. Brunson Campbell and R. J. Carew, op. cit., p. 36. Apparently this work was never published.

13. Addison Walker Reed, op. cit., pp. 183–84. This section has been paraphrased from Reed, for this author feels it is an excellent explanation of the ragtime composition for the layman.

14. Dick Zimmerman. "Interview with Joe Jordan," *Rag Times*, September 1968, p. 6.

15. Rudi Blesh and Harriet Janis. *They All Played Ragtime*, p. 19.

16. Trebor Jay Tichenor. "Missouri Ragtime Revival," *Rag Times*, January 1971, p. 4.

17. The Sedalia *Democrat*, October 16, 1960. Reasons why it was probably not named after the Maple Leaf Club will be discussed later.

18. "The Maple Leaf Route," *Rag Times*, November 1976, p. 7.

19. Bill Mitchell. "The Maple Leaf Rag Story," *Rag Times*, March–April 1969, p. 7.

20. Dick Zimmerman. "Joe Jordan and Scott Joplin," *Rag Times*, November 1968, p. 5.

21. "Original Maple Leaf Club Document Found," *Rag Times*, March 1976, p. 1. This is a recent and important discovery made in 1975 by Naomi Brown, Pettis County, Missouri, Recorder of Deeds. It gave rise to stories in the press that the Maple Leaf Club was not a bawdy house, as legend would have it, but a very respectable gentlemen's club. Actually, it was probably somewhere between the two.

22. The Maple Leaf Club was not listed in any of the city directories.

23. *Rag Times,* May 1974, p. 3. This newspaper item lends support to S. Brunson Campbell's recollections of the Black 400 Club and Joplin's connections with it.
24. Ibid. Neither of these items indicates how long the Maple Leaf Club had been open. Some observers feel the club could hardly have been the subject of the black ministers' ire if it had only been open a month. Others suggest that they could have included it in their indictment even if it was brand new, suspecting that it would be similar to the Black 400 Club.
25. Ibid. Larry Melton, a Joplinophile in Sedalia, found this card in a secondhand bookstore in Sedalia in 1974. It gives rise to the speculation that the Maple Leaf Club might originally have been called Williams' Place and might have been renamed in honor of Joplin's still unpublished rag. S. Brunson Campbell believed the club was named after the tune.
26. The building that housed the club was torn down years ago. In the early 1900s most of the wooden buildings on Main Street were demolished by a tornado. Amazingly, 121 East Main Street remained standing amid the rubble, but it was torn down in the general rebuilding that followed.
27. W. D. Hill. "Saga of Scott Joplin," Sedalia *Democrat,* February 11, 1962.
28. "Missouri Was the Birthplace of Ragtime," St. Louis *Post-Dispatch,* January 18, 1961, p. 137. The article consists primarily of an interview with Carrie Bruggeman Stark, widow of Will Stark. According to Sedalia directories, Stark would move his company and his residence several times in the next fourteen years.
29. Prior to 1974 none of the Stark pre-Joplin publications was known, but early in that year St. Louis ragtime player and historian Trebor Jay Tichenor found a copy of "The Lavada March," by E. J. Stark, copyrighted in 1893.
30. "Missouri Was the Birthplace of Ragtime," St. Louis *Post-Dispatch,* January 18, 1961, p. 137. Some Joplin sources state that John Stark first discovered Joplin when he dropped by the Maple Leaf Club for a drink and heard

the pianist. Impressed with the man's music, Stark invited him to stop by his publishing office the next day, whereupon the encounter with Joplin and his young friend ensued.

31. The contract was witnessed by R. A. Higdon, nothing of whom was known until his daughter, Lucile Higdon, saw an item in the Sedalia *Democrat* about the contract. In a letter to the paper she wrote: ". . . My father had just graduated from Missouri University Law School in 1898, so he had just opened his law office. My father and mother said that Scott Joplin used to play for all their dances, and my dad was such a music lover that when Scott Joplin played the Maple Leaf Rag my dad was so impressed with it, he told Scott 'You should have it published.' But Scott said that 'he didn't know how to do that,' so my father said he'd attend to getting it published for him. I know my father did it as a friend and admirer of the musician, not with any thought of monetary gain. So he interested and secured Stark in publishing the Maple Leaf Rag, and my father handled the contract to make it legal for Joplin . . ." *Rag Times,* November 1975, p. 11.

32. John Stark once wrote: "Scott Joplin left his mark on American music when he first came to our office . . . with the manuscript of the 'Maple Leaf Rag' and 'Sunflower Drag.' He had tried other publishers but had failed to sell them. We quickly discerned their quality, bought them and made a five year contract with Joplin to write only for our firm." Quoted in W. D. Hill, "Saga of Scott Joplin," p. 1. The question of the existence of a contract has been the subject of continuous controversy. Some point to the several compositions Joplin placed with other publishers in the next five years. It is this author's belief, however, that there was such a contract and that Joplin broke it at two crucial periods when he and Stark were disagreeing about the publication of his first two extended works.

33. Dick Zimmerman, op. cit., p. 5.

34. This edition is very rare. Trebor Jay Tichenor has one; it is not known how many are extant.

35. Roy Carew and Private Don E. Fowler. "Scott Joplin: Overlooked Genius," *The Record Changer*, October 1944, p. 10. This statement contradicts the legend that "Maple Leaf Rag" sold 75,000 copies in its first six months and enabled Joplin to cease performing for a living.
36. Ibid., p. 14.
37. S. Brunson Campbell, "The Ragtime Kid (An Autobiography)" (unpublished), Fisk University Library Special Collections, Samuel Brunson Campbell Papers, n.p.
38. Other members of the company were Latisha Howell, whose stage name was Zaorada Tosschatie, Ludie Umbler, Murrte Whitley, Frank Bledsoe, Henry Burres and Lourenda Brown, according to Arthur Marshall, in Rudi Blesh and Harriet Janis, *They All Played Ragtime*, p. 71.
39. S. Brunson Campbell, op. cit., n.p. Some earlier Joplin writers have cited this statement as evidence that "Maple Leaf Rag" was written in 1897, but this author feels Joplin was referring to "Original Rags."
40. S. Brunson Campbell and R. J. Carew, op. cit., p. 37. The authors go on to say: "In those Sedalia days Joplin couldn't foresee that in later years his 'Maple Leaf Rag' would become a standard teaching number, that musicians' unions would use it as a qualifying test for admittance, that Les Copeland, the great ragtime pianist with minstrel shows, would play Joplin rags at a command performance before the King of England."
41. "Missouri Was the Birthplace of Ragtime," St. Louis *Post-Dispatch*, January 18, 1961, p. 137. Earlier Joplin sources state that the Starks moved late in 1901. However, since the firm was listed in the St. Louis City Directory for 1901, it is likely that they moved there the previous year.
42. Gould's St. Louis City Directory, 1901. This, too, belies the immediate popularity of "Maple Leaf Rag."
43. Addison Walker Reed, op. cit., pp. 80–81. In 1971, Reed spoke with Mrs. Mildred Steward, daughter of Arthur Marshall, as well as to relatives and contemporaries of Hayden. All agreed that Joplin and his young protégés worked together on improvisations frequently and contributed equally to their collaborative works.

44. Rudi Blesh and Harriet Janis, op. cit., pp. 52–53.
45. Stark's rapid climb, due to the success of "Maple Leaf Rag," is shown graphically in the St. Louis city directories. Listed as a tuner in 1901, by 1903 he is listed as John Stark & Son, music. In 1905 he is John Stark, President, Music Printing and Publishing Co.; the 1906 listing gives his residence in New York.
46. Letter to the author from Daniel A. Conforti, Executive Assistant, American Brands, Inc., October 13, 1976.
47. Trebor Jay Tichenor says that Perry purchased the rag in 1900, and indeed stylistically it belongs to Joplin's Sedalia period.
48. According to legend, they were married either in Sedalia or St. Louis. However, neither the St. Louis nor the Pettis County Recorder of Deeds has any record of their marriage—or, for that matter, of a later divorce. It is likely that they lived as common-law man and wife.

CHAPTER V: *St. Louis*

1. Gould's St. Louis Directory, 1902. Morgan Town Road is now Delmar Street, and the row house in which the Joplins lived still stands.
2. Passports were not required for American travelers prior to World War I. (Letter to the author from William B. Wharton, Chief, Legal Division, Passport Office, December 21, 1976.) Joplin may have visited Europe later, around 1905, a possibility that is discussed in Chapter VI.
3. Rudi Blesh and Harriet Janis, *They All Played Ragtime*, 1959, p. 101.
4. Gould's St. Louis Directory, 1899, lists Turpin, Thomas M., insp. r 2638 West Chestnut. The 1900 directory lists him as a laborer living at 2221 West Chestnut.
5. No address is given for this saloon in the city directory.
6. Trebor Jay Tichenor, "Chestnut Valley Days," *Rag Times*, November 1971, p. 3.
7. Dick Zimmerman. "Joe Jordan and Scott Joplin," *Rag Times*, November 1968, p. 5.
8. Trebor Jay Tichenor, op. cit., p. 3.

9. Kay C. Thompson, "Lottie Joplin," *The Record Changer*, October 1950, p. 8.

10. Peter Gammond. *Scott Joplin and the Ragtime Era*, p. 127.

11. Rudi Blesh. "Scott Joplin: Black American Classicist," Introduction to *Scott Joplin: Collected Piano Works*, Vera Brodsky Lawrence, ed., p. xxiv.

12. Trebor Jay Tichenor, "The Entertainer," *Rag Times*, July 1974, p. 5.

13. Rudi Blesh and Harriet Janis, op. cit., p. 69. Now that *Treemonisha* has been produced, perhaps this ballet will be performed as well.

14. Freeman later composed a number of operas, and his *Voodoo* is believed to be the first opera written by a Negro, based on a Negro theme, to be performed by a Negro cast on Broadway (1928). Freeman and Joplin knew each other, and Joplin may have been influenced by Freeman's work.

15. Rudi Blesh and Harriet Janis, op. cit., pp. 66–67. Carter's use of "Maple Leaf Club" rather than "Maple Leaf Rag" is an interesting slip. In a later article, Carter states that the piece was named after the Maple Leaf Club, which may be one reason why this legend persists.

16. Called the Rosebud Cafe in some sources, it was called the Rosebud Bar in 1904 advertisements in the St. Louis *Palladium*. Advertised as a distributor for Old Rosebud Whiskey, the club may have derived its name from the liquor brand name.

17. *Rag Times*, November 1971, p. 3. The site is now occupied by a radiator shop.

18. Gould's St. Louis City Directory, 1903, lists Joplin, Scott, music, r. 2117 Lucas Ave. Earlier Joplin sources state that he owned the house. It does not appear that he ever owned a house, either in St. Louis or in New York.

19. Roy Carew discovered a card in the Copyright Office that read: "Class cxx 42461. Feb. 18, 1903. A GUEST OF HONOR, a ragtime opera written and composed by Scott Joplin, published by John Stark and Son." Roy Carew and

Private Don E. Fowler, "Scott Joplin: Overlooked Genius," *The Record Changer,* October 1944, p. 12.

20. Letter quoted in Rudi Blesh and Harriet Janis, op. cit., p. 71.
21. Undoubtedly this article is one source of the erroneous legend that "Maple Leaf Rag" was an immediate hit.
22. It is not known whether Joplin visited Chicago at this time or conducted the publishing arrangements by mail or through a friend in Chicago.
23. Trebor Jay Tichenor. "'Weeping Willow': An Analysis," *Rag Times,* March 1973, p. 4.
24. According to most earlier sources, the baby was born early in 1905. Attempts to locate either a birth or a death certificate for the baby in St. Louis have been fruitless. The placing of the birth two years earlier here results from documentation that in 1904 Joplin was living in Sedalia. This is also the reason why the breakup between Scott and Belle is placed in 1903 here rather than in 1905. That Scott and Belle separated, tried to make up, and conceived the child in the process is unlikely.
25. Rudi Blesh and Harriet Janis, op. cit., pp. 79–80.

CHAPTER VI: *On the Move Again*

1. The New York *Dramatic Mirror,* September 12, 1903, October 17, 1903, and October 24, 1903. According to legend, the opera was also performed once in Sedalia, and that performance, if it did take place, likely occurred on this tour.
2. Interview with Trebor Jay Tichenor by Jan Goldberg, May 1976. Actually, it is not known when these parades began.
3. The article includes a substantial list of people who attended and who assisted Tom Turpin, a list too long to include in the body of the text; it did not mention Joplin. The concentration of the writer on the orderliness of the affair indicates a certain defensiveness; either such affairs were not always orderly or the white population considered them generally rowdy.

4. It would seem that an agreement had been signed to this effect. Otherwise, the Perry company would not have waited to publish the rag.

5. Edwin C. McReynolds. *Missouri: A History of the Cross-roads State,* p. 228.

6. Roy Carew and Private Don E. Fowler. "Scott Joplin: Overlooked Genius," *The Record Changer,* October 1944, p. 11.

7. Now that the identity of Joplin's German mentor is known, it is possible that Ernst either gave him the book or suggested that he buy it. That Joplin owned the book is mentioned in Rudi Blesh's introduction to *Scott Joplin: Collected Piano Works,* p. xxxiv.

8. Trebor Jay Tichenor, " 'The Chrysanthemum': An Analysis," *Rag Times,* September 1974, p. 11.

9. Trebor Jay Tichenor says: "I always thought that the Sedalia tunes had a kind of uncomplicated freshness about them that he later lost. Later, Joplin got much more complicated and emotional in the rags he wrote while he was in St. Louis. As time went on, his writings got more involved, because he'd go from one thing to another—he was always experimenting—he was always changing—year periods—different patterns—always changing—much more than any of the other composers." Interview with Jan Goldberg, May 1976. Undoubtedly, this was due in part to the influence of Alfred Ernst.

10. The cover bears the legend "Entered at Stationer's Hall, London, England," the old way of establishing British copyright. No British edition has ever been found.

11. Trebor Jay Tichenor, "Chestnut Valley Days: An Interview with Charlie Thompson," *Rag Times,* November 1971, p. 3. Tichenor says in this article, ". . . let me assert that I have the utmost faith in Charlie's recall . . . Charlie is very hep and not given to spinning tales."

12. Rudi Blesh and Harriet Janis, op. cit., pp. 79–80.

13. Robert Allen Bradford, "Arthur Marshall: Last of the Sedalia Ragtimers," *Rag Times,* May 1968, p. 8.

14. In *They All Played Ragtime,* by Rudi Blesh and Harriet

Janis, it is stated that Marshall was living at 2900 State
Street (p. 231). If so, he did not list himself in the
Chicago directories. The directories for 1905–7 list an
Arthur Marshall, laborer, at 143 Sedgwick Avenue, but he
may not have been *the* Arthur Marshall. An interesting
possibility is that Robert and Will Joplin preceded Scott to
Chicago. The 1905 directory lists a Robert B. Joplin as living at 2635 Armitage Avenue and a William Joplin, laborer, at 602 West Fifty-ninth Street. In the 1906 and 1907
directories there are no listings for a Robert Joplin. William Joplin is listed at the same address. The only listing
for Scott is in 1906, at 2840 Armour Avenue.

15. Rudi Blesh, "Scott Joplin: Black American Classicist," In-
    troduction to *Scott Joplin: Collected Piano Works*, Vera
    Brodsky Lawrence, ed., p. xxx.
16. Rudi Blesh and Harriet Janis, op. cit., p. 231.
17. Interview with Trebor Jay Tichenor, May 1976. Tichenor
    found advertisements to this effect in St. Louis black
    newspapers.
18. Surviving relatives and friends remember his visiting at
    least twice. Mattie Harris, Scott Joplin's niece, was eighty-
    eight years old in 1976. She remembers Scott's visiting
    when she was in her pre-teens, or around 1900. George
    Mosley was seventy-seven years old in 1976. He has a
    faint recollection of Scott's returning to Texarkana, and
    must remember the 1907 visit. Fred Joplin, Scott's nephew,
    says he remembers a visit in 1907.
19. No death certificate for Florence has as yet been located.
    She is last listed in the Texarkana City Directory of 1902.
    Mattie Harris says she had died by 1904.
20. "The 1939 History," p. 10.
21. Interview with George Mosley, June 1976.
22. Jerry Atkins, "Scott Joplin: Early Days in Texas," *Rag
    Times*, September 1972, p. 3; interview with Jerry Atkins,
    June 1976.
23. Interview with Jerry Atkins, June 1976.
24. Interview with George Mosley, June 1976.
25. Texarkana city directories indicate that the separation oc-
    curred sometime between 1901, when Jiles is listed at 830

Laurel, and 1906, when he is listed at 815 Laurel. Laura Joplin is listed at 830 Laurel in 1905, 1908, and 1910.

26. Ann and John Vanderlee, "The Early Life of Scott Joplin," *Rag Times,* January 1974, p. 2.

27. Interview with Fred Joplin, June 1976: "Now Robert . . . I didn't see him until I went to Chicago, and that was in the early twenties. Now Willie, I never did see him."

28. Ibid.

29. Telephone interview with Mattie Harris, June 1976.

30. Interview with George Mosley, June 1976.

31. Interview with Fred Joplin, June 1976.

32. Rudi Blesh and Harriet Janis, op. cit., pp. 235–37.

33. "The Jess Williams Joplin Story," *Rag Times,* September 1976, p. 9. Aspects of the story are questionable. Williams remembers Joplin as a tall, slender man and as a pianist of some prowess. By most other accounts, Joplin was a small man and not a particularly good pianist. Williams recalls that the meeting took place in 1909, and that Joplin told him that he and his wife had recently broken up; yet Joplin and Belle Hayden had been separated for some years. It is possible that the man who called himself Scott Joplin was an impostor. But it is also possible that to the teen-age Williams he appeared taller than he actually was, and a better pianist than he actually was, and that he was still brooding about Belle. And Williams' recollection just might be off by a couple of years.

34. "Man Who knew Joplin Is the Man of the Hour," *The Washingtonian,* August 11, 1972, p. B1.

35. Kay C. Thompson, "Lottie Joplin," *The Record Changer,* October 1950, p. 8., gives the year 1907. Blesh and Janis say that the year was 1909. S. Brunson Campbell stated that the two were married June 18, 1910. A search of the marriage records for the Borough of Manhattan for 1907, 1909, and 1910 reveals no record of the marriage, and attempts to locate a record of marriage in Washington, D.C., have also proved unsuccessful.

36. Trebor Jay Tichenor, "Missouri Ragtime Revival," *Rag Times,* January 1971, p. 5.

37. New York *Age,* April 4, 1917.

38. Rudi Blesh and Harriet Janis, op. cit., p. 242.
39. Roy Carew and Private Don E. Fowler, op. cit., p. 12.
40. Rudi Blesh, op. cit., p. xxvii.

CHAPTER VII: Treemonisha

1. Interview with Trebor Jay Tichenor, May 1976. John Stark and his son Will failed to forsee the eventual mechanization of music and copyrighted only the sheet music, reserving no rights to either piano rolls or records. In 1961, Will's widow, Carrie Bruggeman Stark, said, "Some people think 'Maple Leaf' and other rags made us rich, but unfortunately that just isn't so. Eventually, the copyrights ran out on the sheet music, and we never made a dime on the thousands of ragtime piano rolls that became popular. Now, of course, it is obvious that Will and his father made a mistake in not protecting all the rights to this early music, but in those early days it was difficult to see just what lay around the corner—musically speaking."
2. "Leo Feist: Ragtime Publisher," *The Metronome*, September 1923, reprinted in *Rag Times*, March 1973, pp. 10–11.
3. Russ Cassidy, "Joseph Lamb: Last of the Ragtime Composers," *Jazz Monthly*, August 1961, p. 6.
4. Rudi Blesh, "Scott Joplin: Black American Classicist," Introduction to *Scott Joplin: Collected Piano Works*, Vera Brodsky Lawrence, ed., p. xxxv.
5. Rudi Blesh and Harriet Janis, *They All Played Ragtime*, p. 204.
6. Russ Cassidy, op. cit., p. 6. After the death of Lottie Joplin in 1953, Lamb told her lawyer that he was willing to pay for the rag, should it be found among her effects, but he received no response.
7. Rudi Blesh and Harriet Janis, op. cit., p. 249.
8. Kay C. Thompson, "Lottie Joplin," *The Record Changer*, October 1950, p. 18. To this author's knowledge, the person and the song have not been identified.
9. William J. Schafer and Johannes Reidel, *The Art of Ragtime*, p. 205.
10. Stark is listed in Trow's General Directory (New York

City) for four years. His business address is the same in all four directories. His various home addresses were as follows: 1906 and 1907, 2321 Old Broadway; 1908, 9 Old Broadway; 1909, 400 Manhattan Avenue (a new apartment building called "The Parthenon").

11. Rudi Blesh and Harriet Janis, op. cit., p. 242.

CHAPTER VIII: *The Last Years*

1. Dick Zimmerman. "Ragtime Recollections," *Rag Times*, May 1968, p. 7.
2. The building still stands and now houses one of Harlem's many religious sects. Next door is the building where the famous nightclub Connie's Inn was once located.
3. Peter Gammond. *Scott Joplin and the Ragtime Era*, p. 148.
4. Trow's General Directory, 1916. Other Joplin sources state that the move to Harlem occurred earlier, and do not mention this first Harlem residence of the Joplins, citing only the address to which they moved the following year.
5. Patterson is not listed in the city directory until 1917 and then at 336 West Fifty-ninth Street.
6. Rudi Blesh and Harriet Janis. *They All Played Ragtime*, pp. 248-9.
7. S. Brunson Campbell, "The Ragtime Kid (An Autobiography)," *Jazz Report*, VI, 1967, n.p. Campbell is the only writer on Joplin who identified the theater; other writers call it simply a "dingy theatre." The Lincoln underwent a change in 1915, from the original movie house established by Mrs. M. C. Downs about 1909 to an enlarged vaudeville house in October 1915. If *Treemonisha* was presented there when it was "dingy," then the performance probably occurred in the spring or early summer of 1915.
8. Orrin Clayton Suthern II, "Minstrelsy in Popular Culture," in *Remus, Rastus, Revolution,* Marshall Fishwick, ed., p. 70.
9. Lynde Denig, "A Unique American Playhouse," *The Theatre* magazine, June 1916, p. 362.
10. Reprinted in "Joplin Gets Second Hit," Dick Zimmerman, *Rag Times*, May 1974, p. 1.

11. Earlier Joplin sources suggest that Scott contracted the disease in New York's Tenderloin. However, the symptoms of dementia paralytica do not arise until at least eight years after the contraction of syphilis, and can remain latent for as long as twenty years. It is more likely that Scott contracted syphilis during his wandering period following the breakup with Belle. It is also likely that he was or had been under treatment. The symptoms described here and later on are conjectural, based on the usual symptoms exhibited in the three stages of dementia paralytica and on the notation on Joplin's death certificate that the onset of the illness occurred one and a half years before his death.

12. Trow's General Directory, 1917: "Joplin, Lottie furn rms 163 W 131st St." They did not own the building, as other sources state. Renting rooms to rent out in turn was a common practice at the time.

13. Rudi Blesh, "Scott Joplin: Black American Classicist," Introduction to *Scott Joplin: Collected Piano Works*, Vera Brodsky Lawrence, ed. p. xxix.

14. Dick Zimmerman, op. cit., p. 7.

15. Interview with Trebor Jay Tichenor, May 1976.

16. To this author's knowledge the music has never surfaced. However, Lottie Joplin mentioned a symphony to Kay Thompson in 1950: "When Scott died, he was composing a ragtime symphony, which he believed would be his most important effort."

17. Kay C. Thompson, "Lottie Joplin," *The Record Changer*, October 1950, p. 18. Some other writers on Joplin have suggested that he was paranoid. However, paranoia is not a usual symptom of dementia paralytica. And, according to Lottie, Scott had good reason to be concerned about his scripts. As she told Thompson, ". . . he was afraid that, if anything happened to him, they might get stolen. In those days, there was a lot of that; more than you might think."

18. Death certificate for Scott Joplin, City of New York, Department of Health, Bureau of Vital Records.

19. Ibid. Cause of death is listed as: Dementia Paralytica—cerebral form. Duration: 1 yr. 6 mos. Contrib. cause:

Syphilis—unknown duration. In the spring of 1977 this author heard that some of Joplin's belongings were still being held at the hospital and made inquiries. However, in a letter dated June 23, 1977, Preston Grier, Associate Director of Manhattan Psychiatric Center, stated that no property that might have belonged to Joplin could be located.

20. "The Great American Composer," reprinted in *Rag Times*, July 1974, p. 24.
21. Kay C. Thompson, op. cit., p. 18.
22. New York *Age*, April 5, 1917. Contrary to legend, there was no large impressive funeral procession, no mourners' cars draped with banners printed with the names of Joplin's most famous rags.
23. Rudi Blesh and Harriet Janis, op. cit., p. 250.
24. Roy Carew and Private Don E. Fowler, "Scott Joplin: Overlooked Genius," *The Record Changer*, October 1944, p. 11.

SELECTED BIBLIOGRAPHY

BOOKS

Allen, W. F., C. P. Ware, and L. M. Garrison. *Slave Songs of the United States.* New York: A. Simpson, 1867. Republished, Oak Publishing Company (paper), 1967.

Blesh, Rudi. *Shining Trumpets.* New York: Alfred A. Knopf, 1958.

———, and Harriet Janis. *They All Played Ragtime.* New York: Grove Press, 1959.

Buerkle, Jack V., and Danny Baker. *Bourbon Street Black.* New York: Oxford University Press, 1973.

Bullock, Henry Allen. *A History of Negro Education in the South.* Cambridge, Mass.: Harvard University Press, 1967.

Carroll, J. M. *A History of Texas Baptists.* Dallas, Tex.: Baptist Standard Publishing Company, 1923.

Charters, Samuel B., and Leonard Kunstadt. *Jazz: A History of the New York Scene.* Garden City, N.Y.: Doubleday, 1962.

Courlander, Harold. *Negro Folk Music U.S.A.* New York: Columbia University Press, 1969.

Davis, William R. *The Development and Present Status of*

Negro Education in East Texas. New York: Teacher's College Press, 1934.

Eby, Frederick. *The Development of Education in Texas.* New York: Macmillan, 1925.

Gammond, Peter. *Scott Joplin and the Ragtime Era.* London: Abacus, 1975.

Ginzburg, Ralph. *One Hundred Years of Lynchings.* New York: Lancer, 1969.

Goldberg, Isaac. *Tin Pan Alley.* New York: Frederick Ungar, 1961.

Haskins, James. *Witchcraft, Mysticism and Magic in the Black World.* Garden City, N.Y.: Doubleday, 1974.

Haskins, Jim, and Hugh F. Butts. *The Psychology of Black Language.* New York: Barnes and Noble, 1973.

Hentoff, Nat, and Albert J. McCarthy, eds. *Jazz.* New York: Da Capo Press, 1975.

Katz, Bernard, ed. *The Social Implications of Early Negro Music in the United States.* New York: Arno Press and the New York *Times,* 1969.

Katz, William Loren, ed. *The American Negro: His History and Literature.* New York: Arno Press and the New York *Times,* 1969.

King, Edward. *The Great South.* Hartford, Conn.: American Publishing Company, 1875.

Lawrence, Vera Brodsky, ed. *Scott Joplin: Collected Piano Works.* Introduction, "Scott Joplin: Black American Classicist," by Rudi Blesh, New York: New York Public Library, 1971.

Locke, Alain. *The Negro and His Music: Negro Art Past and Present.* New York: Arno Press and the New York *Times,* 1969.

McReynolds, Edwin C. *Missouri: A History of the Crossroads State.* Norman, Okla.: University of Oklahoma Press, 1962.

Meinig, D. W. *Imperial Texas: An Interpretative Essay in Cultural Geography.* Austin, Texas.: University of Texas Press, 1969.

Osofsky, Gilbert. *Harlem: The Making of a Ghetto.* New York: Harper & Row, 1968.

Ramsey, Frederic, Jr. *Been Here and Gone.* New Brunswick, N.J.: Rutgers University Press, 1960.

Reed, Addison Walker. *The Life and Works of Scott Joplin.* Unpublished doctoral thesis, University of North Carolina, Chapel Hill, 1973.

Rice, Lawrence D. *The Negro in Texas: 1874–1900.* Baton Rouge, La.: Louisiana State University Press, 1971.

Roach, Hildred. *Black American Music.* Boston: Crescendo Publishing, 1973.

Sargeant, Winthrop. *Jazz: Hot and Hybrid.* New York: Da Capo Press, 1975.

Schafer, William J., and Johannes Reidel. *The Art of Ragtime.* Baton Rouge, La.: Louisiana State University Press, 1973.

Southern, Eileen. *The Music of Black Americans: A History.* New York: Norton, 1971.

Stearns, Marshall W. *The Story of Jazz.* New York: Oxford University Press, 1958.

Sterling, Dorothy, ed. *The Trouble They Seen: Black People Tell the Story of Reconstruction.* Garden City, N.Y.: Doubleday, 1976.

Swint, Henry Lee. *The Northern Teacher in the South.* New York: Octagon Press, 1967.

Williams, Martin, ed. *Jazz Panorama.* New York: Collier Books, 1964.

ARTICLES AND PERIODICALS

New York *Age*, April 5, 1917.

"A Musical Novelty," *American Musician*, June 24, 1911.

Arnold, W. H., Sr. "Historical Statement of Texarkana, Arkansas, to February 7, 1917." *Arkansas Historical Quarterly*, Vol. 5, No. 4, 1946, pp. 341–53.

Brockhoff, Dorothy. "Ragtime Professor," *Washington University* magazine, Summer 1972, p. 35.

Campbell, S. Brunson. "Ragtime Begins: Early Days with Joplin Recalled," *The Record Changer*, March 1948, p. 8.

——. "The Ragtime Kid (An Autobiography)" (edited version reprinted), *Jazz Report*, Vol. VI, 1967, n.p.

——, and R. J. Carew. "Sedalia, Missouri: Cradle of Ragtime," *The Record Changer*, May 1945, p. 3; June 1945, p. 36.

Carew, R. J. "Treemonisha," *The Record Changer*, October 1946.

———, Roy, and Private Don E. Fowler. "Scott Joplin: Overlooked Genius," *The Record Changer*, September 1944, p. 12; October 1944, p. 11.

Cassidy, Russ. "Joseph Lamb: Last of the Ragtime Composers," *Jazz Monthly*, August 1961, pp. 4–7.

Collier, James Lincoln. "The Scott Joplin Rag," New York *Times Magazine*, September 21, 1975, p. 19.

Daily, Georgia. "Childhood Friend Remembers Joplin," Texarkana *Gazette*, May 6, 1976.

Denig, Lynde. "A Unique American Playhouse," *The Theatre* magazine, June 1916, p. 362.

"Emancipation Day," Sedalia *Democrat*, August 4, 1899.

Giddins, Gary. " 'Treemonisha' from on High Breaks Loose," *Village Voice*, May 24, 1976, p. 90.

Goodwin, Noel. "Ragtime Reckoning," *About the House*, Vol. 4, No. 7, Christmas 1974, pp. 12–17.

Hill, W. D. "Saga of Scott Joplin," Sedalia *Democrat*, February 11, 1962, p. 1.

"Joplin, 'Father of Ragtime,' Honored," Indianapolis *News*, November 26, 1975.

"Joplin's Black Gold," *Newsweek*, September 22, 1975, p. 62.

Kupferberg, Herbert. "Joplin's Opera Finally Makes It Big," *National Observer*, September 27, 1975.

"Man Who Knew Joplin Is the Man of the Hour," *The Washingtonian*, August 11, 1972, p. B1.

"Missouri Was the Birthplace of Ragtime," St. Louis *Post-Dispatch*, January 18, 1961, p. 137.

Nation, The, Vol. 4. May 30, 1867, pp. 432–33.

New York *Age*, March 5, 1908, May 19, 1910, April 24, 1913, August 7, 1913, August 14, 1913, September 7, 1916, March 29, 1917, April 5, 1917.

New York *Dramatic Mirror*, September 12, October 17, October 24, 1913.

"Orr School Is Nominated for National Historic Site," Texarkana *Gazette*, May 2, 1976.

"Ragtime Music was Born in Sedalia." The Sedalia *Democrat*. October 16, 1960.

Rag Times, 1967–77.

Rich, Alan. "Scott Joplin's 20/20 Vision," *New York* magazine, November 3, 1975, p. 83.

"St. Louis and Scott Joplin," St. Louis *Post-Dispatch*, February 2, 1972.

"School Named for Scott Joplin," New York *Amsterdam News*, February 8, 1975, p. D-11.

"Scott Joplin Awarded a Special Pulitzer Prize," Texarkana *Gazette*, May 5, 1976.

"Scott Joplin and the Ragtime Revival," New York *Record World*, July 6, 1974, p. 20.

"Scott Joplin Dies of Mental Trouble," New York *Age*, April 5, 1917.

"Scott Joplin: From Rags to Opera," *Time*, September 15, 1973, p. 85.

"Scott Joplin: Renascence of a Black Composer of Ragtime and Grand Opera," *Negro History Bulletin*, January 1974, p. 188.

Suthern, Orrin Clayton II. "Minstrelsy in Popular Culture," in Marshall Fishwick, ed. *Remus, Rastus, Revolution*. Bowling Green, Ohio: Bowling Green University Press, n.d.

Thompson, Kay C. "Lottie Joplin," *The Record Changer*, October 1950, p. 8.

———. "Rag-time and Jelly Roll," *The Record Changer*, April 1948, p. 8.

Tichenor, Trebor Jay. "Missouri's Role in the Ragtime Revolution," *Missouri Historical Bulletin*. Vol. XVII, April 1960, p. 239.

"To Play Ragtime in Europe," St. Louis *Post-Dispatch*, February 28, 1901.

Vanderlee, Ann and John, "Scott Joplin's Childhood Days in Texarkana," *Rag Times*, November 1973, p. 5.

———. "The Early Life of Scott Joplin," *Rag Times*, January 1974, p. 2.

EPHEMERA

Documents

American Statistical Association, New Series No. 61, March 1903. "The Negroes of St. Louis," by Lillian Brandt. New York Public Library, Microfilm No. LAC 40138.

Selected Bibliography

Census Records, Bowie and Cass Counties, Texas, 1850, 1860, 1870, 1880, Collections of the National Archives, Washington, D.C., The New York Public Library, The Schomburg Center for Research in Black Culture, The Texas State Library.

Chicago City Directory, 1905–7, Collection of the Chicago Historical Society.

City of New York, Department of Health, Bureau of Vital Records, certificate of death for Scott Joplin.

First Annual Report of Public Free Schools of the City of Texarkana, Texas, 1887.

Fisk University Library Special Collections, Nashville, Tennessee, Samuel Brunson Campbell Papers.

Duncan, Green C., letter to Mrs. M. E. Duncan, University of Texas Archives, Green C. Duncan Papers.

Gould's St. Louis City Directory, 1884–1907, Collection of the Missouri Historical Society, St. Louis, Missouri.

Hooks family genealogy, compiled January 1970, by Mrs. Arthur Jennings, Texarkana.

McCoy's Sedalia City Directory, 1894–1901, Collection of the Sedalia Public Library.

New York City Real Estate Record, 1909–22, Collection of the Museum of the City of New York.

New York City real estate records, Hall of Records, Surrogates Court and Municipal Reference Library.

Simmons and Kernodle's Pettis County and Sedalia City Directory, 1883–84.

State of Arkansas, State Board of Health, Bureau of Vital Statistics, certificate of death for Jiles Joplin.

Texarkana City Directory, 1899–1924, Collection of the Texarkana Historical Society.

Texas Gazetteer and Business Directory, 1882–83, Standard Directory Service, Texarkana, Tex.

Trow's General Directory, New York City, 1900–22, Collection of the Museum of the City of New York.

U. S. Census Records, Kentucky—various counties—1830, 1840, 1850, Collection of the New York Public Library, Schomburg Center for Research in Black Culture.

Pamphlets

Chandler, Barbara Overton, and J. Ed. Howe. "History of Texarkana and Bowie and Miller Counties, Texas-Arkansas." Shreveport, Louisiana, 1939. Collection of the Texarkana Historical Society and Museum.

"Dedication of State of Texas Historical Commission Official Marker: Scott Joplin," 1976.

"History of Texarkana, Texas," no author, no date, Collection of the New York Public Library.

Holland, Lucille. "The Texarkana Story, 1873–1948." Texarkana, Arkansas-Texas, n.d., Collection of the New York Public Library.

Jennings, Nancy Moores Watts. "Moores or Mooresville and Harrison Chapel Cemetery, Bowie County, Texas," Texarkana, Texas, 1967.

———. "Texarkana Pioneer Family Histories," Texarkana Pioneers Association, 1961, Collection of the New York Public Library.

———, and Mary L. S. Phillips, compilers. "Texarkana Centennial Historical Program," Texarkana, Arkansas-Texas, 1973.

Liner notes. "The Sound of Harlem," *Jazz Odyssey*, Vol. III. Frank Driggs, producer. Columbia Jazz Archive Series, 1964.

Meadows, Emma Lou. "De Kalb and Bowie County History and Genealogy," De Kalb, Texas, 1968, Collection of the New York Public Library.

Playbill, "Scott Joplin's 'Treemonisha,'" Uris Theatre, 1975.

"The 1939 History," Dunbar High School, Texarkana, Arkansas-Texas.

INDEX

Index

780.92 Haskins, James
HAS
      Scott Joplin

DATE			
3/5			
JAN 2 1 1980			
0/13			
MAR 11 1981			
MAY 23 1983			
MAY 10 1983			